The Gen X Series

ENGLISH OLYMPIAD 7

Useful for English Olympiads Conducted at School, National & International Levels

Author
Suparna Sengupta

Peer Reviewer
P. Shyamla

Strictly According to the Latest Syllabus of English Olympiad

Published by:

F-2/16, Ansari road, Daryaganj, New Delhi-110002
☎ 23240026, 23240027 • *Fax:* 011-23240028
✉ info@vspublishers.com • 🌐 www.vspublishers.com

 Online Brandstore: amazon.in/vspublishers

Regional Office : Hyderabad
5-1-707/1, Brij Bhawan (Beside Central Bank of India Lane)
Bank Street, Koti, Hyderabad - 500 095
☎ 040-24737290
✉ vspublishershyd@gmail.com

Follow us on:

BUY OUR BOOKS FROM: | AMAZON | FLIPKART |

© Copyright: *V&S* PUBLISHERS
ISBN 978-93-579407-5-7
New Edition

DISCLAIMER

While every attempt has been made to provide accurate and timely information in this book, neither the author nor the publisher assumes any responsibility for errors, unintended omissions or commissions detected therein. The author and publisher makes no representation or warranty with respect to the comprehensiveness or completeness of the contents provided.

All matters included have been simplified under professional guidance for general information only, without any warranty for applicability on an individual. Any mention of an organization or a website in the book, by way of citation or as a source of additional information, doesn't imply the endorsement of the content either by the author or the publisher. It is possible that websites cited may have changed or removed between the time of editing and publishing the book.

Results from using the expert opinion in this book will be totally dependent on individual circumstances and factors beyond the control of the author and the publisher.

It makes sense to elicit advice from well informed sources before implementing the ideas given in the book. The reader assumes full responsibility for the consequences arising out from reading this book.

For proper guidance, it is advisable to read the book under the watchful eyes of parents/guardian. The buyer of this book assumes all responsibility for the use of given materials and information.

The copyright of the entire content of this book rests with the author/publisher. Any infringement/transmission of the cover design, text or illustrations, in any form, by any means, by any entity will invite legal action and be responsible for consequences thereon.

Publisher's Note

General Trade and Mass Appeal books across various genres have helped **V&S Publishers** to gain widespread popularity. In a short span of 10 years, we have successfully published more than 1000 titles across 9 languages in our 50 subject categories. Being into the publishing business for about 40 years, we have always been a dynamic publishing house, with a massive distribution network, across India; including E-commerce platforms.

Understanding the need of inculcating knowledge and developing a spirit of healthy competition amongst students to make them ready for the world outside schools and colleges; we created Olympiad Series under the **GEN X SERIES Imprint** which, owning to its rich content and unique representation became popular amongst students, in no time. The motivation is not to improve marks in terms of numbers, but is to make sure that the students are already prepared to face competitive environment with respect to college admissions and cracking various entrance examinations, while ensuring their conceptual clarity.

Published for classes 1-10 across subjects English, Mathematics, Science, Computers, General Knowledge, the books are unlike any other in the market and are written in a guidebook pattern and exhaustively include examples and Multiple-Choice Questions.

Here, we present the latest Edition of **ENGLISH OLYMPIAD CLASS 7**.

Unique Features of the book are as follows:

- Authored by Subject Matter Experts' and Peer reviewed by School Principals and HOD's for the respective subjects
- Books based on principles of Applied Psychology and Bloom's Taxonomy
- Suited for Olympiad Examinations held at School level, National level & International Level irrespective of organizing body.
- The only Olympiad Book in India written in Guidebook Pattern with Concise Theory, images and illustrations.
- Exhaustively include Examples, MCQs, Subjective Questions, and HOTS with Answer Keys & Solutions.
- Multiple Model Papers for thorough practice also given inside the book with solutions.
- OMR sheets appended at the end of the book for simulating exam environment.

Besides, we are also planning to launch an App very soon for the Olympiad preparation which further testifies our constant endeavor to keep up with student demands. We have made sure to closely follow syllabus patterns of not only Olympiad conducting bodies but also education boards & organizations like CBSE and NCERT, to make sure that our books prove useful to students; helping them to boost their academic performance in schools as well.

P.S. While every care has been taken to ensure the correctness of the content, if you come across any error, howsoever minor, do not hesitate to discuss with teachers while pointing that out to us in no uncertain terms.

We wish you All the Best!

DISTINCTIVE

WHY OLYMPIADS?
Olympiads are just like competitive exams; conducted by various bodies at national and international levels. The aim is to experience a competitive examination at the school level and also to help students to discover their interest acrss subjects like English, Mathematics, Science and General Knowledge.

WHY V&S OLYMPIADS?
We at V&S Publishers aim to build an avid-reading student audience. Hence, our resolve is to follow an innovative pedagogic pattern which would help students to navigate through the book with utmost ease and comfort. Crisp theory practical examples and illustrations keep our book interactive and comprehensive.

01 LEARNING OBJECTIVES
They list the whole chapter as subtopics, helping the teachers to guide children in a step-by-step manner.

02 DID YOU KNOW
Enhance your knowledge by getting acquainted with some amazing facts across various subjects like science, Mathematics and English.

03 MULTIPLE CHOICE QUESTIONS
MCQs act as an excellent learning aid, helping you to understand and work on your mistakes.

04 THINGS TO REMEMBER
A quick recap of the chapter in a summarized format helps in faster revision along with conceptual clarity.

05 HOTS
The High Order Thinking Questions aim to help the student to solve Application-based questions and gain practical understanding of the subject.

FEATURES

06 SUBJECTIVE QUESTIONS
Help to place the knowledge gained in orderly fashion by using "WH" questions, mostly in the form of bullet points.

07 ACHIEVER'S SECTION
Offers a quick revision of the book along with some new facts for the students to discover.

08 A SET OF OMR SHEETS
To allow the student to practice question in an exam-like format which would help them to get the "feel" of how Olympiad exams take place.

09 MODEL TEST PAPERS
Two model test papers are provided at the end of each book, which help the student to test the knowledge which they have gained after thorough reading of all chapters.

10 ANSWER KEY & SOLUTIONS
Detailed Answer Key along with explanations aid the pupil to indentify, understand the mistakes they make during the course of Olympiad preparation.

COMPLEMENT SCHOOL SYLLABI
The syllabi across all Olympiad examination closely follow the pattern of academic books. Hence, they not only provide a competitive examination experience, but also help to revise topics for school examinations as well, while strengthening conceptual precision.

ENHANCEMENT OF ANALYTICAL & LOGICAL REASONING
Practicing analytical ability questions, not only helps in developing intellectual ability but also plays a vital role in building critical thinking ability which helps an individual to think about a question or a crisis like situation in day to day life; from all aspects and directions.

Note to Parents

Dear Parents,

Olympiad examinations come with a plethora of advantages. First and foremost among such advantages is the application of knowledge studied, in the form of multiple-choice questions. It helps the child not only to step away from rote learning, but also helps them to exhibit their competencies across various subjects.

In addition to this, Olympiads help the student to understand the importance of revision and practice, and to imbibe upon these practices; which also prove useful in academic performance of the child.

The Olympiads are conducted across multiple subjects, and help the child to recognize their field of interest, thereby encouraging the students to make a career in the field where they can excel the most.

However, cognitive development of a child is not just limited to the four walls of classroom. Following steps can be encouraged by you, to ensure their ward is able to grasp various concepts with ease or lesser difficulty:

- **Eat a balanced diet:** Ensure intake of vitamins and minerals to keep you active. Include fruits and super foods like millet in your diet to ensure healthy functioning of organs. Huge intake of junk food should be avoided.
- **Indulge in outdoor activities:** Outdoor games break the monotony of life. Play your heart out in greenery to keep yourself alert, active and fit.
- **Sleep well:** A sound sleep of 7-8 hours refreshes the brain and makes it ready to understand new topics with more clarity. A sleep derived person faces difficulty in doing even the simplest tasks of day to day life.
- **Reduce your Screen time:** More screen time leads to not only weakening of eyesight but decreases concentration span. Regulated Screen time should be encouraged
- **Do not hesitate to raise a hand:** Having a doubt in class? Do not hesitate to ask your parents or teachers. This ensures more Conceptual Clarity and hence leads to Application based understanding of various subjects and topics.
- **Teach and Learn:** No need to do rote-learning. Once you understand a topic teach or explain it to your friends, siblings and parents. It brings clarity and ensures the child does his revision this way.
- **Keep smiling:** A positive attitude promotes a growth mindset and encourages the child to be more inquisitive and try to learn something new, everyday!

HAPPY LEARNING!

Contents

SECTION 1: WORD AND STRUCTURE KNOWLEDGE

1. Spellings and Collocation — 9
2. Synonyms, Antonyms, Homonyms and Homophones — 19
3. Analogies — 32
4. One Word — 35
5. Phrasal Verbs and Idioms, Modals, Word Order — 41
6. Nouns and Pronouns — 51
7. Verbs and Adverbs — 57
8. Adjectives — 64
9. Articles and Prepositions — 69
10. Conjunctions and Punctuations — 76
11. Tenses — 92
12. Voices and Narration — 96
13. Vocabulary — 113

SECTION 2: READING COMPREHENSION

1. Reading Comprehension – I — 121
2. Reading Comprehension – II — 129

SECTION 3: SPOKEN AND WRITTEN EXPRESSIONS

Spoken and Written Expressions — 135

SECTION 4: ACHIEVERS' SECTION

Some Thoughtful Questions — 139
Model Test Paper–1 — 142
Model Test Paper–2 — 146

ANSWER KEYS (Access Content online on Dropbox) — 150
Appendix — 161

SECTION 1
WORD AND STRUCTURE KNOWLEDGE

Spellings and Collocation

Learning Objectives : In this chapter, students will learn about:
- Rules of Spelling
- Importance of Collocations
- Types of Collocations

CHAPTER SUMMARY

Some basic rules of spellings help us understand the formation of words. On the basis of these rules, we learn to derive various spellings and words.

Rules of Spelling

Rule 1: Usually 'i' precedes 'e' except after 'c'.
Example
believe, achieve, (except after c), receive, ceiling (but not when 'c' is sounded like 'sh') ancient, proficient; not when sounded like 'a') eight, beige

Rule 2: Change 'y' to 'ies'. When the word ends in a vowel + y, just add 's'.
Example
key — keys
delay — delays (because we can't have three vowels in a row 'delaies')
trolley — trolleys

If the word has a consonant before the 'y', take off the 'y' and add 'ies'
baby — babies
company — companies
difficulty — difficulties

Rule 3: Add 'es' to the words ending in -s, -ss, -z -ch -sh -x. This is added to stop the plural 's' clashing with these letters and it softens the 's' sound to a 'z' sound.
Example
bus — buses
business — businesses
watch — watches
box — boxes
quiz — quizzes

Rule 4: Double the last letter of the word. When a word has one syllable + one vowel next to one consonant, we double up the final consonant with a vowel suffix.
Example
put — putting
tap — tapping
big — bigger
shop — shopper/shopping
quiz — quizzes
swim — swimming
sit — sitter
fat — fatten, fattening, fatter, fattest
big — biggest

This happens in longer words when the stress is on the final syllable.
begin — beginner, beginning
refer — referring, referred
occur — occurring, occurred, occurrence

> **TRIVIA**
> The original name for butterfly was flutterby.

Rule 5: Drop the 'e' rule. We usually drop the final silent "e" when we add vowel suffix endings.
Example
write + ing = writing
hope + ed = hoped
excite + able = excitable

sense + ible = sensible
opposite + ion = opposition
imagine + ation = imagination
We keep the **'e'** if the word ends in – **ce** or – **ge** to keep a soft sound, with able/ous.
courage + ous = courageous
notice + able = noticeable
outrage + ous = outrageous
manage + able = manageable

Rule 6: Change 'y' to 'i' when adding suffix endings. If a word ends in a consonant + Y, the Y changes to i (unless adding endings with "i" -ing -ish, which already begins with an i).
Beauty + ful = beautiful, beautify, beautician
ready = readily, readiness
happy + ness = happiness, happily, happier, happiest
dry = dried, BUT drying, dryish
angry + er = angrier, angriest, angrily
defy = defies, defied, but defying
pretty = prettier, prettiest but prettyish
apply = applies, applied but applying

Rule 7: Changing '-f' to '-ves' or '-s'.
Most words ending in '-f' or '-fe', change their plurals to '-ves'.

Example

calf	—	calves
life	—	lives
half	—	halves
wife	—	wives
knife	—	knives
shelf	—	shelves
leaf	—	leaves
thief	—	thieves
loaf	—	loaves
yourself	—	yourselves

Exception

scarf	—	scarfs
dwarf	—	dwarfs
wharf	—	wharfs
handkerchief	—	handkerchiefs

Words ending in **-ff**, just add **-s** to make the plural.

cliff	—	cliffs
scuff	—	scuffs
toff	—	toffs
sniff	—	sniffs

Nouns which end in two vowels with 'f' usually form plurals in the normal way, with just an -s.

chief	—	chiefs
spoof	—	spoofs
roof	—	roofs
oaf	—	oafs

Exception

thief	—	thieves
leaf	—	leaves

Rule 8: Words ending in -ful. The suffix –ful is always spelt with single l.

Example
grate + ful = grateful
faith + ful = faithful
hope + ful = hopeful
beautiful (notice 'y' becomes 'i')

Rule 9: By adding 'ly' to them. When we add -ly to words ending in –ful, we have double letters.
gratefully
faithfully
hopefully
We also add -ly to the words ending in 'e'.
love + ly = lovely
like + ly = likely
live + ly = lively
BUT not truly (true + ly). This is a common misspelled word.
We change the ending **'e'** to **'y'** in these 'le' words.

gentle	—	gently
idle	—	idly
subtle	—	subtly

Rule 10: When we add 'all' to the beginning of words, we drop the 'l'.
all + so = also
all + most = almost
although
always
almighty
already

Collocation

A collocation is a combination of words that are commonly used together; the simplest way of describing collocations is to say that they 'just sound right' to native English speakers. Other combinations that may mean the same thing would seem 'unnatural'. Collocations include noun phrases like ' stiff wind' and 'weapons of mass destruction', phrasal verbs such as 'to get together' and other stock phrases such as 'the rich and famous'.

Importance of Collocations

Language becomes more natural and is more easily understood.

- You will have alternative and richer ways of expressing yourself.
- It is easier for our brains to remember and use language in chunks or blocks rather than as single words.

Tips to Learn Collocations

- Be aware of collocations, and try to recognize them when you see or hear them.
- Treat collocations as single blocks of language. Think of them as individual blocks or chunks; for example, learn strongly support, not strongly + support.
- When you learn a new word, write down other words that collocate with it (remember rightly, remember distinctly, remember vaguely, remember vividly).
- Read as much as possible. Reading is an excellent way to learn vocabulary and collocations in context and naturally.
- Revise what you learn regularly. Practise using new collocations in context as soon as possible after learning them.
- Learn collocations in groups that work for you. You could learn them by topic (time, number, weather, money, family) or by a particular word (take action, take a chance, take an exam).
- You can find information on collocations in any good learner's dictionary. And you can also find specialized dictionaries of collocations.

Types of Collocation

There are several different types of collocation. The following are seven main types of collocation in simple sentences.

1. Adverb + Adjective
Examples

We entered a **richly decorated** room.

Are you **fully aware** of the implications of your action?

2. Adjective + Noun
Examples

The doctor advised him to take **regular exercise**.

The Titanic sank on its **maiden voyage**.

He was writhing on the ground in **excruciating pain**.

3. Noun + Noun
Examples

Let's give Mr. Verma a **round of applause**.

The **ceasefire agreement** came into effect at 11 am.

4. Noun + verb
Examples

The lion started to roar when it heard the **dog barking**.

Snow was falling as our **plane took off**.

The bomb went off when he started the **car engine**.

5. Verb + Noun
Examples

The prisoner was hanged for **committing murder**.

I always try to do my homework in the morning, after **making my bed**.

6. Verb + Expression with preposition
Examples

We had to return home because we had **run out of money**.

At first her eyes filled with horror, and then she **burst into tears**.

Their behaviour was enough to **drive anybody to crime**.

7. Verb + Adverb
Examples

Mary **whispered softly** in John's ear.

I **vaguely remember** that it was growing dark when we left.

8. Common Collocations

It is important to learn collocations, because they are important for naturalisation of one's speech. Besides, they broaden one's scope for expression.

The following is a list of collocations to help you get started:

Collocations with the verb 'do'	
Do me a favour	Do the cooking
Do the housework	Do the shopping
Do the washing up	Do your best
Do your hair	

Collocations with the verb 'have'	
Have a good time	Have a bath
Have a drink	Have a haircut
Have a holiday	Have a problem
Have a relationship	Have lunch
Have sympathy	

Collocations with the verb 'break'	
Break the law	Break a leg
Break a promise	Break a record
Break someone's heart	Break the ice
Break the news to someone	Break the rules

Collocations with the verb 'take'	
Take a break	Take a chance
Take a look	Take a rest
Take a seat	Take a taxi
Take an exam	Take notes
Take someone's place	

Collocations with the verb 'make'	
Make a difference	Make a mess
Make a mistake	Make a noise
Make an effort	Make money
Make progress	Make room
Make trouble	

Collocations with the verb 'catch'	
Catch the bus	Catch a ball
Catch a cold	Catch a thief
Catch fire	Catch sight of
Catch someone's attention	Catch someone's eye
Catch the flu	

| Collocations with the verb 'pay' ||

Pay respect	Pay a fine
Pay attention	Pay by credit card
Pay cash	Pay interest
Pay someone a visit	Pay the bill
Pay the price	
Collocations with the verb 'keep'	
Keep the change	Keep a promise
Keep a secret	Keep an appointment
Keep calm	Keep in touch
Keep quiet	Keep someone's place
Collocations with the verb 'save'	
Save yourself the trouble	Save electricity
Save energy	Save money
Save someone a seat	Save someone's life
Save something to a disk	Save time
Collocations with the verb 'go'	
Go bald	Go abroad
Go astray	Go blind
Go bankrupt	Go fishing
Go crazy	Go missing
Go mad	Go out of business
Go online	Go quiet
Go overseas	Go sailing
Collocations with the verb 'come'	
Come under attack	Come close
Come direct	Come early
Come first	Come into view
Come last	Come late
Come on time	Come prepared
Come right back	Come to a decision
Come to an agreement	Come to an end
Come to a standstill	Come to terms with
Come to a total of	
Collocations with the verb 'get'	
Get a job	Get a life
Get hold of	Get a shock
Get angry	Get divorced
Get drunk	Get frightened

Spellings and Collocation

Get home	Get lost
Get married	Get permission
Get ready	Get started
Get the impression	Get upset
Get wet	Get worried
Collocations related to 'time'	
Bang on time	Dead on time
Free time	From dawn till dusk
Great deal of time	Early/late 15th century
Make time for	Next few days
Past few weeks	Right on time
Run out of time	Time goes by
Time passes	Waste time
Collocations related to Business English	
Annual turnover	Keep in mind
Break off negotiations	Close a deal
Close a meeting	Come to the point
Dismiss an offer	Draw a conclusion
Draw your attention to	Launch a new product
Go bankrupt	Go into partnership
Make a profit/loss	

How to learn collocations

Notice collocations
When you're reading, look at which words go together. If you have to write about a topic, try to find a newspaper article or a magazine article about that topic and look at the phrases that the journalist uses. You'll often see the same phrases again and again.

Use a collocation dictionary
Collocations Dictionary is a very useful book. You can look up any word and see which other words are usually used with it. If you don't have a collocation dictionary, a learner's dictionary will give you several good example phrases for each word, as well as telling you which prepositions and so on the word is used with.

When you study vocabulary, learn whole phrases, not single words. For example, it's better to learn 'to insist on doing something' rather than just 'insist'. If you need to learn 'effort', make sure you study 'make an effort'.

Learn vocabulary
Learn phrases (groups of words) rather than single words. You can learn new words by seeing them often when you read, so you should also study new words seriously.

Make use of flashcards
There are really the best way to learn new words by a long way. You can use paper flashcards (make or buy them) or a flashcard computer program. Write the new English word (in a phrase, of course!) on one side and either the translation in your language or the meaning in easy English on the other side. Then test yourself often. It's best to look at the meaning and try to remember the new phrase, rather than the opposite.

- When a word has one syllable + one vowel next to one consonant, we double up the final consonant with a vowel suffix.
- If a word ends in a consonant + Y, the Y changes to i (unless adding endings with "i" -ing -ish, which already begins with an i).
- A collocation is a combination of words that are commonly used together.
- It is important to learn collocations, because they are important for naturalisation of one's speech. Besides, they broaden one's scope for expression.

PRACTICE EXERCISE

I. Choose the correct option to replace the incorrect spellings/words given in the following sentences.

1. We reached the hotel quiet late and could not find any accommodation.
   (a) reachd   (b) quite
   (c) accomodation (d) hotale

2. The chameleon is known for its ability to camoflage itself.
   (a) chamileon   (b) abbility
   (c) nown   (d) camouflage

3. This year our school has decided to focus on the envirement and use of recycled products.
   (a) school   (b) decidead
   (c) environment   (d) recicled

4. The cat knocked down the vace and looked at its owner with mischievous eyes.
   (a) nocked   (b) vase
   (c) mischevous   (d) oner

5. We are having a workshop where we are going to learn correct pronounciation of some difficult words.
   (a) wokshop   (b) corect
   (c) pronunciation (d) difficult

II. Choose the correctly spelled word/option for the given expressions.

1. To stop something from burning
   (a) extinguish   (b) estinguish
   (c) extanguish   (d) ecstinguish

2. A feeling of appreciation or thanks
   (a) grotitude   (b) gratatude
   (c) gratitude   (d) gratitute

3. To make very angry or annoy
   (a) exasparate   (b) exasperate
   (c) ecsasperate   (d) exasparade

4. Made up of parts that are different
   (a) hetrogeneous (b) hatrogeneous
   (c) heterogenious (d) heterogeneous

5. An area of water that moves in circle
   (a) whirlpull   (b) whorlpool
   (c) whirlpool   (d) wirlpool

6. The usual mood of a person
   (a) desposition   (b) disposition
   (c) disposetion   (d) dispossession

7. Hard to find
   (a) allusive   (b) ellusive
   (c) alusive   (d) elusive

8. The main person or thing
   (a) principle   (b) principel
   (c) principal   (d) princepal

9. To use words that mean the opposite
   (a) sarcism   (b) sarkasm
   (c) sarcasn   (d) sarcasm

10. Easily hurt or harmed
    (a) valnerable   (b) vulnerabale
    (c) vulnerable   (d) vulnarable

11. Friendly or polite
    (a) amicable   (b) amikable
    (c) amicabale   (d) emicable

12. Childish
    (a) juvanile   (b) juvenile
    (c) juivenile   (d) juvenil

13. Feeling ashamed or foolish in front of others
    (a) embarass   (b) embrace
    (c) embarrass   (d) embarace

14. Strong disapproval
    (a) condemnation (b) condamnation
    (c) condaimnation (d) condemnition

15. Not moving
    (a) stationery   (b) stationary
    (c) stationury   (d) stationory

III. Choose the incorrect spelling from the given options.

1. (a) recieving   (b) paragraph
   (c) fierce   (d) badge

2. (a) artificial   (b) traiter
   (c) anxiety   (d) ejection

3. (a) community   (b) abandone
   (c) implicate   (d) principal

4. (a) paranoid   (b) deprivation
   (c) horrifying   (d) wimsical

5. (a) academic   (b) exception
   (c) miniature   (d) cinnaman

6. (a) recitation   (b) affirmative
   (c) constelation (d) qualifying

7. (a) hypotheses   (b) despondent
   (c) mosquitoes   (d) participete

8. (a) bookshelves (b) conjecture
    (c) farmacist (d) defendant
9. (a) abducted (b) coruption
    (c) advice (d) balloon
10. (a) confiscate (b) elastisity
    (c) typhoon (d) unison

IV. Choose the correct option to fill the blanks in the following sentences.

1. The meeting took almost five hours so it was impossible to_____ attention all the time.
    (a) Pay (b) Paid
    (c) Have paid (d) None of these
2. The problem is difficult to_____ under control.
    (a) Keeping (b) Kept
    (c) Keep (d) None of these
3. It took us all day to clean up the office after the burglary - the thieves _____ a terrible mess.
    (a) Has made (b) Will make
    (c) Made (d) None of these
4. I don't think we should _____ a decision yet; we should wait.
    (a) Has made (b) Make
    (c) Will make (d) None of these
5. Only 31% of the students who_____ the final exam passed it.
    (a) Taken (b) Taking
    (c) Took (d) None of these
6. I think we should look for a new supplier - the one we have at the moment _____ us too many problems.
    (a) Causes (b) Caused
    (c) Will cause (d) None of these
7. Could you _____ me a favour and post these letters on your way home?
    (a) Did (b) Do
    (c) Done (d) None of these
8. I've told him ten times that he's got the wrong telephone number. I'll _____ crazy if he calls again.
    (a) Go (b) Gone
    (c) Going (d) None of these
9. The company offers its employees free language training but not many people _____ advantage of it.
    (a) Take (b) Took
    (c) Taken (d) None of these
10. Our personnel assistant is leaving next month - she's _____ a baby.
    (a) Expected (b) Expect
    (c) Expecting (d) None of these
11. You have to _____ risks if you go into business.
    (a) Do (b) Make
    (c) Get (d) Take
12. You should always confirm appointments you _____ on the phone by sending a follow-up email.
    (a) Do (b) Make
    (c) Get (d) Take
13. We _____ a lot of business in China.
    (a) Do (b) Make
    (c) Get (d) Take
14. You will need to _____ better qualifications if you want to have a good career.
    (a) Do (b) Make
    (c) Get (d) Take
15. With one of our study programmes you can study and continue working to _____ practical experience.
    (a) Do (b) Make
    (c) Get (d) Take
16. When someone phones to _____ a complaint, you need to keep calm and sympathise with them as much as possible.
    (a) Do (b) Make
    (c) Get (d) Take
17. You need to _____ a lot of training to become a good programmer.
    (a) Do (b) Make
    (c) Get (d) Take
18. I'm hoping that if I work hard, I'll _____ promotion soon. It would be great to have a higher position with more responsibility.
    (a) Do (b) Make
    (c) Get (d) Take
19. We _____ a break every two hours.
    (a) Do (b) Make
    (c) Get (d) Take
20. When I _____ my job well, my boss always tells me how pleased she is with my work.
    (a) Do (b) Make
    (c) Get (d) Take

Spellings and Collocation

HOTS

I. **DIRECTIONS: Find out correct meaning of the following collocations from the given options.**

1. Money Laundering
   (a) the crime of processing stolen money through a legitimate business or sending it abroad to a foreign bank, to hide the fact that the money was illegally obtained.
   (b) storing money
   (c) stealing money
   (d) spending money

2. A Round of Applause
   (a) praising somebody
   (b) the noise made by a group of people clapping their hands to show approval
   (c) a token of gratitude
   (d) a note of appreciation

3. Make Coffee
   (a) preparing coffee
   (b) serving coffee
   (c) put on a pot of coffee to serve to drink yourself or serve others
   (d) taking coffee

4. Flesh and blood
   (a) human beings
   (b) severe bloody fighting
   (c) matter of common concern
   (d) member of your family

5. Frenetic competition
   (a) friendly contest
   (b) serious and energetic effort to defeat a person, group or organisation in a contest
   (c) old rivalry
   (d) open fighting

II. **In each sentence below, one word has been printed in bold type which is wrongly spelt. Choose the correctly spelt word for each.**

6. If you give **succor** to someone who is suffering or in difficulties, it means you help them.
   (a) sucour   (b) succour
   (c) succuor   (d) succor

7. DIRECTIONS: In each sentence below, one word has been printed in bold type which is wrongly spelt. Choose the correctly spelt word for each. The bank manager asked him to check his **superanuation** scheme.
   (a) superannuation
   (b) superenuation
   (c) superennuation
   (d) superenation

8. Whatever the **vicisitudes** of her past life, Priya now seems to have come through.
   (a) visitudes   (b) vicissitudes
   (c) vicitudes   (d) viscitudes

9. Lata Mangeskhar has thousands of songs in her **repertoare**.
   (a) repertoir   (b) rapertoir
   (c) repertoire   (d) repertare
   Answer: C

10. If you have an **acquaintence** with someone, you have met them and you know them.
    (a) acquaintance   (b) acquaintence
    (c) acquintance   (d) acquentence

Synonyms, Antonyms, Homonyms and Homophones

Learning Objectives : In this chapter, students will learn about:
- Some common Synonyms and Antonyms
- Some common Homonyms and Homophones

CHAPTER SUMMARY

Synonyms

Synonyms are the words that have a similar meaning. By using them, we can avoid repetition of words in speech and writing.

The following is a list of synonyms.

Word	Synonym
abandon	leave
abode	dwelling
abduct	kidnap
abbreviate	shorten
abrupt	sudden
abroad	overseas
abundant	plentiful
accident	mishap
accomplish	achieve
acute	sharp
accurate	exact
accuse	blame
acquire	obtain
act	deed
adequate	enough
adhere	stick to
admire	adore
affectionate	loving
aged	elderly
aid	help
allow	permit
ally	friend
alter	change
altitude	height
amazement	wonder
ample	plenty
ancient	old
anger	fury
anxious	worried
assemble	gather
astonished	surprised
attire	dress
attract	entice
awful	terrible
authority	power
bad	evil
big	large
blank	empty
broad	wide

ban	prohibit	desire	wish
beg	plead	desperate	hopeless
behavior	conduct	destiny	fate
brave	courageous	detest	hate
brief	short	difficult	hard
calamity	disaster	diminish	lessen
calm	quiet	disclose	reveal
capture	seize	disperse	scatter
cause	reason	drowsy	sleepy
centre	middle	doubtful	uncertain
cunning	crafty	dull	boring
cease	stop	eager	keen
chance	opportunity	edible	eatable
chaos	disorder	educate	teach
check	inspect	elevate	raise
chilly	cold	elude	escape
choose	select	embrace	hug
circular	round	eminent	famous
coarse	rough	encircle	surround
combine	join	endeavor	attempt
compel	force	enemy	foe
competition	contest	enormous	huge
conceal	hide	enquire	ask
conclude	end	entire	whole
confess	admit	escape	flee
courteous	polite	essential	important
cruel	unkind	eternal	forever
cure	heal	evidence	proof
custom	habit	excess	surplus
dangerous	risky	exterior	outside
damage	harm	false	untrue
damp	moist	famous	noted
deadly	fatal	fashion	style
deceive	cheat	fatal	deadly
deficiency	shortage	fatigue	tiredness
demonstrate	show	fault	error

fear	terror	legitimate	legal
feeble	weak	loathe	hate
find	discover	lodging	accommodation
fortunate	lucky	lazy	indolent
frank	honest	little	small
frightened	scared	loyal	faithful
gain	profit	mad	insane
gap	hole	malady	disease
gather	collect	mammoth	huge
gay	cheerful	meagre	scanty
gaze	stare	memorable	unforgettable
genuine	real	minimum	least
glad	happy	mischievous	naughty
glance	look	miserable	wretched
gleaming	shining	mistake	error
grave	serious	modern	new
grief	sorrow	moist	wet
halt	stop	mull	consider
haste	hurry	neat	tidy
help	assist	necessary	essential
hinder	obstruct	noted	well-known
humorous	funny	notorious	infamous
illegal	unlawful	obscene	indecent
imitate	copy	occasion	event
incorrect	wrong	odd	strange
inevitable	unavoidable	odour	smell
interfere	meddle	often	frequently
interior	inside	oppose	object
invaluable	priceless	option	choice
join	unite	origin	source
jovial	cheerful	peaceful	tranquil
jump	leap	peak	summit
just	fair	penetrate	pierce
lament	grieve	perceive	see
lean	thin	peril	danger
leave	depart	peruse	read

Synonyms, Antonyms, Homonyms and Homophones

petite	small	scent	fragrance
petty	trivial	scorn	despise
plain	simple	seldom	rarely
plunge	dive	significant	important
ponder	think	shout	yell
powerful	strong	sight	vision
predict	foretell	slender	slim
pretty	beautiful	soar	rise
probe	investigate	squander	waste
procure	obtain	stationary	still
prompt	quick	stern	strict
purpose	intention	suitable	appropriate
quaint	queer	summon	call
quantity	amount	surrender	yield
quit	stop	thrust	push
rage	anger	thrill	excite
raiment	clothes	transparent	clear
rank	position	trust	believe
rapid	quick	try	attempt
rare	uncommon	unique	exceptional
reckless	rash	vanish	disappear
recollect	remember	velocity	speed
reluctant	unwilling	victory	triumph
remote	distant	vital	important
rescue	save	wrath	anger
residence	house	weak	feeble
respond	reply		
reveal	show		
rich	wealthy		
ridiculous	absurd		
riot	revolt		
roam	wander		
row	quarrel		
rude	impolite		
safe	secure		
scatter	disperse		

Antonyms

Antonyms are the words that mean the opposite of each other.

Example

correct – incorrect, ancient – modern, agree – disagree, large – small

Following are some common examples of antonym.

Word	Antonym
absent	present
accept	decline, refuse
admit	deny

against	for	day	night
alive	dead	dead	alive
ally	enemy	decrease	increase
ancient	modern	definite	indefinite
appear	disappear, vanish	despair	hope
arrive	depart	disappear	appear
ascend	descend	diseased	healthy
attractive	repulsive	downwards	upwards
backward	forward	dry	moist, wet
beautiful	ugly	dusk	dawn
begin	end	east	west
bent	straight	empty	full
better	worse, worst	end	begin, start
black	white	even	odd
bless	curse	export	import
borrow	lend	external	internal
boy	girl	fail	succeed
build	destroy	famous	unknown
borrow	lend	fast	slow
boundless	limited	feeble	strong, powerful
brighten	fade	find	lose
calm	windy, troubled	float	sink
capable	incapable	fore	aft
careful	careless	fold	unfold
cheerful	sad, discouraged	found	lost
clever	stupid	frequent	seldom
close	far, distant	for	against
clumsy	graceful	full	empty
combine	separate	gentle	rough
comfort	discomfort	giant	tiny, small, dwarf
conceal	reveal	give	receive, take
cool	warm	gloomy	cheerful
courage	cowardice	good	bad, evil
crooked	straight	great	tiny, small
compulsory	voluntary	guest	host
dangerous	safe	happy	sad

Synonyms, Antonyms, Homonyms and Homophones

hard	soft	minor	major
harsh	mild	miser	spendthrift
healthy	diseased, ill, sick	more	less
heavy	light	near	far, distant
here	there	never	always
high	low	night	day
hinder	help	no	yes
horizontal	vertical	none	some
humble	proud	obedient	disobedient
ill	healthy, well	offer	refuse
important	trivial	old	new
include	exclude	open	closed, shut
inferior	superior	optimist	pessimist
inner	outer	outer	inner
intelligent	stupid, unintelligent	past	present
interior	exterior	peace	war
internal	external	plentiful	scarce
join	separate	poetry	prose
just	unjust	possible	impossible
knowledge	ignorance	powerful	weak
landlord	tenant	private	public
last	first	pure	impure
lawful	unlawful, illegal	raise	lower
leader	follower	rare	common
lenient	strict	real	fake
less	more	right	left, wrong
like	dislike, hate	rough	smooth
limited	boundless	safe	unsafe
long	short	satisfactory	unsatisfactory
lose	find	scatter	collect
loud	quiet	serious	dangerous
low	high	shallow	deep
mad	happy, sane	sick	healthy, ill
many	few	singular	plural
maximum	minimum	slim	fat, thick
merry	sad	sober	drunk

some	none
sour	sweet
straight	crooked
stop	go
strong	weak
sunny	cloudy
sweet	sour
tall	short
them	us
thick	thin
tiny	big, huge
top	bottom
transparent	opaque
truth	lie
unfold	fold
unqualified	qualified
up	down
upstairs	downstairs
useful	useless
vanish	appear
victory	defeat
visible	invisible
war	peace
weak	strong
white	black
win	lose
within	outside
rapid	slow

Homonyms and Homophones
Homonyms are the words that have the same spelling and pronunciation, but differ in meaning.
Example
Bear (to bear a child)
Bear (an animal)
Homophones are the words that have the same pronunciation, but are different in meaning and spellings. They may or may not have the same spelling. That is the only difference they have with homonyms.

Example
ate – eight, bare – bear, birth – berth
So, all homonyms are homophones but all homophones are not homonyms.

TRIVIA

The English language is said to be one of the happiest languages in the world – oh, and the word "happy" is used 3 times more often than the word "sad"!

Some common homophones are given below.

Word	Homophone
Aisle (passage way)	Isle (island)
Aloud	Allowed
Air	Heir
Ale (a drink)	Ail (illness)
Ate	Eight
Altar (table used in ceremonies)	Alter (change)
Ball	Bawl (cry)
Bare	Bear
Beech (a tree)	Beach
Bean	Been
Bee	Be
Berry	Bury
Birth	Berth
Blew	Blue
Boar	Bore
Bored	Board
Brake	Break
Buy	By/bye
Bouy (a floating object)	Boy
Bough (branch of a tree)	Bow
Bell	Belle (a girl)
Ceiling	Sealing

Synonyms, Antonyms, Homonyms and Homophones

Cell	Sell	Lain	Lane
Cent	Scent/sent	Leak	Leek
Check	Cheque	Loan	Lone
Cord (a kind of rope)	Chord (musical note)	Loot	Lute
Coarse (rough)	Course	Lessen	Lesson
Deer	Dear	Made	Maid
Die	Dye	Mail	Male
Eye	I	Main	Mane
Earn	Urn (a vase)	Meat	Meet
Fair	Fare	Medal	Meddle
Feat	Feet	Missed	Mist
Find	Fined	None	Nun
Flea	Flee	Oar	Ore
Forth	Fourth	One	Won
Flew	Flu	Pail	Pale
Fur	Fir	Pain	Pane
Flour	Flower	Pair	Pear
Gait	Gate	Patience	Patients
Grate	Great	Peace	Piece
Groan	Grown	Peal	Peel
Hail	Hale	Plain	Plane
Hair	Hare	Pore	Pour
Hall	Haul	Pray	Prey
Heal	Heel	Principal	Principle
Hear	Here	Rain	Reign
Heard	Herd	Rap	Wrap
Higher	Hire	Reed	Read
Hymn	Him	Right	Write
Hole	Whole	Ring	Wring
Hour	Our	Road	Rode
Idle	Idol	Role	Roll
Key	Quay	Route	Root
Knight	Night	Rose	Rows
Know	No	Sale	Sail
Knot	Not	Scene	Seen
Lead	Led	Sea	See

Stair	Stare		Waist	Waste
Steal	Steel		Wait	Weight
Tail	Tale		Way	Weigh
Their	There		Weak	Week
Threw	Through		Wear	Where
Throne	Thrown		Witch	Which
Tide	Tied		Wood	Would
To	Two/too		Yoke	Yolk
Vain	Vein		Your	You're
Vale	Veil			

MUST REMEMBER

- Synonyms are the words that have a similar meaning. By using them, we can avoid repetition of words in speech and writing.
- Antonyms are the words that mean the opposite of each other.
- Homonyms are the words that have the same spelling and pronunciation, but differ in meaning.
- Homophones are the words that have the same pronunciation, but are different in meaning and spellings.

PRACTICE EXERCISE

I. Choose the correct synonym for the given word.

1. Kind
   - (a) nice
   - (b) wild
   - (c) funny
   - (d) best
2. Glad
   - (a) broken
   - (b) happy
   - (c) open
   - (d) round
3. Fast
   - (a) clear
   - (b) main
   - (c) clean
   - (d) quick
4. Shiny
   - (a) extra
   - (b) careful
   - (c) bright
   - (d) angry
5. Big
   - (a) large
   - (b) many
   - (c) next
   - (d) only
6. Noisy
   - (a) first
   - (b) loud
   - (c) afraid
   - (d) small
7. Final
   - (a) last
   - (b) first
   - (c) heavy
   - (d) small
8. Tired
   - (a) kind
   - (b) fatigued
   - (c) ready
   - (d) angry
9. Merry
   - (a) safe
   - (b) happy
   - (c) upset
   - (d) angry
10. Unhappy
    - (a) playful
    - (b) alive
    - (c) sad
    - (d) angry
11. Similar
    - (a) correct
    - (b) different
    - (c) alike
    - (d) unequal
12. Smart
    - (a) dumb
    - (b) wide
    - (c) intelligent
    - (d) old
13. Weird
    - (a) strange
    - (b) great
    - (c) unhealthy
    - (d) typical
14. Scared
    - (a) happy
    - (b) sad
    - (c) angry
    - (d) afraid
15. Sure
    - (a) likely
    - (b) doubtful
    - (c) certain
    - (d) smart
16. Fair
    - (a) just
    - (b) large
    - (c) loose
    - (d) unbalanced
17. Hilarious
    - (a) smart
    - (b) funny
    - (c) small
    - (d) large
18. Amazing
    - (a) irregular
    - (b) crazy
    - (c) incredible
    - (d) equal
19. Difficult
    - (a) soft
    - (b) easy
    - (c) hard
    - (d) old
20. Packed
    - (a) alone
    - (b) light
    - (c) crowded
    - (d) heavy

II. Choose the correct synonym to replace the underlined word in the following sentences.

1. After watching the alien movie, Parth started believing that one by one everyone would be <u>abducted</u> by aliens.
   - (a) kidnapped
   - (b) shortened
   - (c) blamed
   - (d) obtained
2. Sarah could not believe her mother would actually get her all the things she wanted for her birthday. She kept staring in <u>wonder</u>.
   - (a) plentiful
   - (b) sudden
   - (c) amazement
   - (d) enough
3. It is never a good idea to pick up a fight with the persons in <u>authority</u>. You never know what they are capable of.
   - (a) large
   - (b) power
   - (c) reason
   - (d) middle
4. I hate it when someone gives away the <u>ending</u> of the book I am still reading.
   - (a) story
   - (b) cheat
   - (c) reveal
   - (d) conclusion
5. It's easier to <u>teach</u> children than to teach adults.
   - (a) attempt
   - (b) educate
   - (c) bright
   - (d) discover
6. You are <u>fortunate</u> enough to have such a loving family.

(a) cheerful (b) happy
(c) lucky (d) serious

7. It is hard to imagine him involved in something <u>illegal</u>.
   (a) unlawful (b) wrong
   (c) priceless (d) fair

8. The hills were so <u>peaceful</u>, so different from the busy streets of everyday life.
   (a) queer (b) simple
   (c) trivial (d) tranquil

9. A winter trek up these mountains is not for the <u>reckless</u> and faint-hearted.
   (a) wealthy (b) careless
   (c) strong (d) excited

10. The price of milk has <u>soared</u> in the last month.
    (a) risen (b) pushed
    (c) cleared (d) wasted

III. Choose the correct antonym for the given word.

1. Happy
   (a) disturbed (b) mad
   (c) sad (d) afraid
2. Strong
   (a) thin (b) young
   (c) weak (d) light
3. Beautiful
   (a) expensive (b) hostile
   (c) ugly (d) brave
4. Rare
   (a) painful (b) creepy
   (c) normal (d) common
5. Tiny
   (a) puny (b) large
   (c) small (d) miniscule
6. Easy
   (a) fine (b) fast
   (c) hard (d) strong
7. Low
   (a) here (b) middle
   (c) there` (d) high
8. Sick
   (a) dizzy (b) energetic
   (c) upset (d) well
9. Loose
   (a) super (b) tight
   (c) sticky (d) strong
10. Dark
    (a) colourful (b) heavy
    (c) light (d) smooth

11. Least
    (a) less (b) more
    (c) equal (d) most
12. West
    (a) south (b) north
    (c) east (d) straight
13. Right
    (a) hard (b) wrong
    (c) correct (d) wicked
14. Near
    (a) long (b) away
    (c) far (d) close
15. Late
    (a) heavy (b) soon
    (c) long (d) early
16. Thick
    (a) worn (b) old
    (c) dirty (d) thin
17. Cold
    (a) cool (b) hot
    (c) easy (d) low
18. Similar
    (a) present (b) different
    (c) important (d) secret
19. Safe
    (a) dangerous (b) important
    (c) terrible (d) busy
20. Skinny
    (a) fat (b) large
    (c) small (d) chubby

IV. Choose the correct homophone for the given word.

1. Weather
   (a) whether (b) wither
   (c) writer (d) wether
2. Some
   (a) sun (b) sum
   (c) son (d) song
3. Pour
   (a) peer (b) pier
   (c) pore (d) port
4. Waste
   (a) waist (b) wait
   (c) vest (d) west
5. Rain
   (a) ring (b) ran
   (c) run (d) reign
6. Seem
   (a) seen (b) seam
   (c) scene (d) sin

7. Stare
   - (a) stark
   - (b) star
   - (c) stir
   - (d) stair
8. Tail
   - (a) tall
   - (b) till
   - (c) tale
   - (d) tell
9. Threw
   - (a) through
   - (b) three
   - (c) tree
   - (d) true
10. Yoke
    - (a) york
    - (b) oak
    - (c) yolk
    - (d) woke
11. Right
    - (a) bright
    - (b) night
    - (c) writ
    - (d) write
12. Sail
    - (a) sale
    - (b) sell
    - (c) shell
    - (d) shall
13. Root
    - (a) wrought
    - (b) rout
    - (c) route
    - (d) rude
14. Pale
    - (a) pill
    - (b) pail
    - (c) pall
    - (d) pelt
15. Hoard
    - (a) hood
    - (b) heard
    - (c) herd
    - (d) horde

V. Fill in the blanks with the correct option.

1. The donkey _____ when I tried to ride it.
   - (a) braid
   - (b) brayed
   - (c) bred
   - (d) bread
2. I have to take a _____ to workplace because my car is being repaired.
   - (a) bus
   - (b) buss
   - (c) bust
   - (d) buzz
3. My friend is leaving the city; I have to say _____ to her.
   - (a) by
   - (b) bye
   - (c) buy
   - (d) bi
4. Please _____ some bread when you go to the grocery store.
   - (a) by
   - (b) bye
   - (c) buy
   - (d) bi
5. My sister made a beautiful _____ soup for dinner last night.
   - (a) karate
   - (b) carat
   - (c) karat
   - (d) carrot
6. I was the midnight _____ who woke you with my phone call.
   - (a) collar
   - (b) caller
   - (c) killer
   - (d) cooler

7. Humans cannot live without _____.
   - (a) air
   - (b) heir
   - (c) err
   - (d) ire
8. I want to take a vacation and go to an exotic _____.
   - (a) aisle
   - (b) I'll
   - (c) isle
   - (d) oil
9. We will have to _____ your dress so it fits properly.
   - (a) alter
   - (b) altar
   - (c) halter
   - (d) elter
10. Ask your question _____ if you want an answer.
    - (a) allowed
    - (b) hallowed
    - (c) aloud
    - (d) alert
11. You will _____ several trucks if you take the highway.
    - (a) past
    - (b) puss
    - (c) piss
    - (d) pass
12. My grandfather has a great deal of common _____.
    - (a) sins
    - (b) sense
    - (c) since
    - (d) sync
13. Tom has been collecting comic books _____ he was ten years old.
    - (a) sins
    - (b) sense
    - (c) since
    - (d) cents
14. It took so long, because we lost our ____.
    - (a) weigh
    - (b) way
    - (c) whey
    - (d) wee
15. Although I feel no pain, the wound will take some time to _____.
    - (a) heal
    - (b) hell
    - (c) heel
    - (d) he'll
16. The lion _____ on deer mostly.
    - (a) praise
    - (b) preys
    - (c) prays
    - (d) press
17. The policeman had to _____ the thief by the arm.
    - (a) sees
    - (b) seas
    - (c) seize
    - (d) cease
18. It takes _____ to tango.
    - (a) too
    - (b) two
    - (c) to
    - (d) toe
19. What are you planning to _____ for tonight's party?
    - (a) wear
    - (b) ware
    - (c) where
    - (d) whirr
20. The _____ of us have been friends since school.
    - (a) fore
    - (b) for
    - (c) fur
    - (d) four

HOTS

I. Fill in the blanks with correct antonym of the word(s) given in the brackets.

1. The country is _____ in natural resources. (scarce)
    (a) abundant (b) present
    (c) kind (d) good
2. Risking his own life to save the puppy was a _____ act. (cowardly)
    (a) sweet (b) kind
    (c) nice (d) brave
3. I am always skeptical about _____ money to people. I have had a few bad experiences. (borrowing)
    (a) accepting (b) lending
    (c) encouraging (d) good
4. He gazed _____ longingly at the plane that flew miles over his head. (downward)
    (a) sideways (b) right
    (c) upward (d) left
5. His lack of technical _____ kept him from being promoted. (ignorance)
    (a) knowledge (b) skills
    (c) seniors (d) followers
6. We have _____ control over our emotions but we can certainly be in control of our actions. (boundless)
    (a) limited (b) strict
    (c) unjust (d) external
7. Nothing in this world is _____. (temporary)
    (a) expensive (b) favourable
    (c) good (d) permanent
8. We reached the theatre and found that our seats had been _____. (vacant)
    (a) cleaned (b) removed
    (c) occupied (d) stolen
9. Jennifer was wearing a _____ diamond necklace, but no one realized it. (real)
    (a) fake (b) beautiful
    (c) shiny (d) awesome
10. Honesty, kindness and patience are some of his _____. (vices)
    (a) talents (b) virtues
    (c) qualities (d) skills

II. Choose the correct option for the given word.

1. Waste (homonym)
    (a) waist (b) wait
    (c) vest (d) west
2. Root (homonym)
    (a) wrought (b) rout
    (c) route (d) rude
3. Fair (synonym)
    (a) just (b) large
    (c) loose (d) unbalanced
4. Similar (antonym)
    (a) present (b) different
    (c) important (d) secret
5. Mark the synonym of the words given below: Valour
    (a) Cowardice (b) Wise
    (c) Courage (d) Beautiful

Analogies

Learning Objectives : In this chapter, students will learn about:
- Concept of Analogy
- Types of Analogy

CHAPTER SUMMARY

An analogy shows the relationship between two pairs of words. At first glance, the words in an analogy may seem to have nothing to do with each other, but the words are always logically related. Both pairs of words have the same kind of relationship. To solve an analogy, we need to find that relationship.

The most commonly used noun is "time".

Kinds of Analogy

The word pairs in an analogy can have one of these types of relationships:

- **Antonyms:** The words that have opposite meanings.

  Example
  big: small :: rich: poor
  right: wrong :: tall: short

- **Synonyms:** The words that have same or similar meanings.

  Example
  rapid: quick :: pretty: beautiful
  fashion: style :: false: untrue

- **Part to whole:** One word is a part or piece of the other

  Example
  arm: body :: chapter: book
  toe: foot :: nose: face

- **Item to category:** One word names something that falls into the group named by the other word

  Example
  milk: beverage :: sparrow: bird
  pizza: food :: shirt: clothes

- **Descriptive:** One word describes another.

  Example
  blue: sky :: hard: diamond
  round: ball :: long: pencil

- **Function:** One word is used to complete or carry out an action.

  Example
  fork: eat :: pan: cooking
  shovel: dig :: knife: cut

➡ An analogy shows the relationship between two pairs of words.

PRACTICE EXERCISE

I. Choose the correct word/option that completes the given analogy.

1. sun: hot :: ice: _____
   (a) cold   (b) cubes
   (c) water   (d) melt
2. finger: hand :: petal: _____
   (a) stem   (b) flower
   (c) garden   (d) bike
3. eye: see :: ear:
   (a) here   (b) hearing aid
   (c) hear   (d) song
4. saw: cut :: hammer:
   (a) screwdiver   (b) pound
   (c) chainsaw   (d) screw
5. author: writing :: artist:
   (a) painting   (b) reading
   (c) typing   (d) beauty
6. kitchen: house :: keyboard:
   (a) computer   (b) bedroom
   (c) wires   (d) classroom
7. city: state :: state:
   (a) country   (b) continent
   (c) world   (d) town
8. alive: dead :: awake:
   (a) asleep   (b) ill
   (c) old   (d) life
9. smart: clever :: stupid:
   (a) dumb   (b) irritating
   (c) intelligent   (d) quick
10. airplane: flying :: sailboat:
    (a) pilot   (b) sailing
    (c) swimming   (d) fishing
11. child: family :: student:
    (a) class   (b) teacher
    (c) parents   (d) brother
12. bed: sleeping :: pool:
    (a) lifeguard   (b) snoring
    (c) swimming   (d) billiards
13. clock: time :: thermometer:
    (a) temperature   (b) fever
    (c) mercury   (d) illness
14. sad: happy :: bored:
    (a) gloomy   (b) tired
    (c) exciting   (d) angry
15. wing: bird :: fin:
    (a) frog   (b) bat
    (c) duck   (d) fish
16. beautiful: ugly :: boy:
    (a) pretty   (b) girl
    (c) handsome   (d) good
17. awful: horrible :: interesting:
    (a) fascinating   (b) boring
    (c) terrible   (d) commonplace
18. scissors: cut :: pen:
    (a) ink   (b) write
    (c) paper   (d) exam
19. priest: preaching :: doctor:
    (a) curing   (b) medicine
    (c) church   (d) hospital
20. second: minute :: minute:
    (a) week   (b) season
    (c) hour   (d) year
21. Delhi: India :: Paris:
    (a) Mumbai   (b) Kolkata
    (c) France   (d) London
22. whisker: cat :: fangs:
    (a) bird   (b) goat
    (c) snake   (d) lizard
23. dog: puppy :: cat:
    (a) pet   (b) whiskers
    (c) mother   (d) kitten
24. pretty: beautiful :: thin:
    (a) slender
    (b) fat
    (c) chubby
    (d) handsome
25. push: pull :: give:
    (a) donate   (b) lend
    (c) share   (d) take
26. pilot: fly :: driver:
    (a) sail   (b) drive
    (c) ride   (d) run
27. chimney: smoke :: faucet:
    (a) water   (b) burn
    (c) flow   (d) cold
28. tongue: taste :: nose:
    (a) stink   (b) wrinkle
    (c) sniff   (d) smell

Analogies

29. day: night :: deep:
    (a) sunlight (b) bright
    (c) afternoon (d) shallow
30. letter: word :: word:
    (a) envelope
    (b) sentence
    (c) mailbox
    (d) homework

II. **Choose the correct option. [Hint: which of these sentences make sense?]**

1. (a) A house is used to move.
   (b) A car is used to talk.
   (c) A fork is used to eat.
   (d) A pen is used to read.
2. (a) Birds live in a nest.
   (b) Cows live in a river.
   (c) Bears live in a hotel.
   (d) Dogs live in the forest.
3. (a) A sunny day lacks friends.
   (b) A windy day lacks clothes.
   (c) A rainy day lacks umbrella.
   (d) A cloudy day lacks sunlight.
4. (a) A cat is a part of a dog.
   (b) A branch is a part of a tree.
   (c) A school is part of a truck.
   (d) A table is a part of a chair.
5. (a) Ears are used to hear.
   (b) Hair is used to think.
   (c) Toes are used to talk.
   (d) Eyes are used to smell.
6. (a) Horses are a type of music.
   (b) Jeans are a type of pants.
   (c) Bicycles are a type of plant.
   (d) Roses are a type of food.
7. (a) Cheap is the opposite of expensive.
   (b) Small is the opposite of little.
   (c) Big is the opposite of large.
   (d) Rich is the opposite of wealthy.
8. (a) A bird is a type of animal.
   (b) A fish is a type of colour.
   (c) A human is a type of computer.
   (d) A bag is a type of furniture.
9. (a) Wood is hard.
   (b) Paper is alive
   (c) Ice-cream is cold.
   (d) Cotton is hard.
10. (a) A star is used to run.
    (b) A cup is used to drink.
    (c) An animal is used to jump.
    (d) A pan is used to sweep.

HOTS

DIRECTIONS: In each of the following questions find out of the alternative which will replace the blank.

1. Film : Audience : : _____ : _____.
   (a) Novel: Criticism
   (b) Television: Transmission
   (c) Hero : Heroicism
   (d) Radio: Listener
2. Perfection : Flow :: _____ : _____.
   (a) Careless: Mistake
   (b) Anonymity: Identity
   (c) Employee : Colleague
   (d) Book : Notebook
3. Affirm : Hint :: _____ : _____.
   (a) Pardon : Charge (b) Reject: Refer
   (c) Charge: Insinuate (d) Deny : Speak
4. Fable : Didactic :: _____ : _____
   (a) Sermon : Lengthy (b) Myth: Legendary
   (c) Anecdote : Witty (d) Epic: Comic
5. Paper : Papyrus :: _____ : _____.
   (a) Concrete : Adobe
   (b) Cement: Building
   (c) Brick: Wall
   (d) Wood: Furniture

One Word

Learning Objectives : In this chapter, students will learn about:
- ✓ Usage of One Word

CHAPTER SUMMARY

The key to good writing and speech often means to use less number of words to say the same number of things. 'One word' or shorter words help us replace worded expressions and phrases with just a single one. The following are a few examples of one word.

TRIVIA

The words we use repeatedly during conversation even if they don't add meaning to what you are saying are called "crutch words". Commonly used crutch words – "Actually", "like", "basically", "anyway".

Phrase/Expression	One Word
The life story of a man	Biography
The life story of a man written by himself	Autobiography
A four-legged animal	Quadruped
An animal with two legs	Biped
A person who hates mankind	Misanthrope
A man who does good to others	Philanthropist
Showing kindness and compassion for mankind	Humanitarian
One who does not believe in god	Atheist
One who believes there is only one god	Monotheist
One who is over enthusiastic	Fanatic
One who habitually looks at the bright side of life	Optimistic
One who habitually looks at the dark side of life	Pessimistic
One who always find fault with others	Cynic
One who eats excessively	Glutton
One who spends too much	Spendthrift

One who spends minimum	Miser
A good judge of art, food, etc.	Connoisseur
One who cannot be corrected	Incorrigible
One who can use both hands equally well	Ambidextrous
One who speaks two languages well	Bilingual
One who always talks about himself	Egotist
One of strange, unusual habits	Eccentric
One who is difficult to please	Fastidious
One who never tires	Indefatigable
A plant, animal or man living on another's efforts/earning	Parasite
A great lover of books	Bibliophile
One who walks in sleep	Somnambulist
One who destroys works of art	Vandal
One who is talented in many spheres	Versatile
One who is new to a job	Novice
One who eats human flesh	Cannibal
One who is proficient in many languages	Linguist
One who cannot be defeated	Invincible
The sound that cannot be heard	Inaudible
The object that cannot be seen	Invisible
That cannot be believed	Incredible
That cannot be removed	Indelible
That cannot be satisfied	Insatiable
That cannot be explained	Inexplicable
That cannot be copied	Inimitable
That cannot be changed or withdrawn	Irrevocable
Something which is bound to happen	Inevitable
That which never fails	Infallible
Which cannot be repaired	Irreparable
Which quickly catches fire	Inflammable
One who cannot read or write	Illiterate
Food which is not fit to be eaten	Inedible
A work published after the author's death	Posthumous

Persons living in the same age	Contemporaries
Animals equally at home at land and in water	Amphibians
A person with a long experience in his profession	Veteran
A person belonging to all parts of the world	Cosmopolitan
Something which is out of date	Obsolete
All in agreement	Unanimous
Work done of one's own accord	Voluntary
Things happening at the same time	Simultaneous
Things not connected with the main subject	Irrelevant
A speech delivered without preparation	Extempore
Something attempted for the first time	Maiden
A match/contest in which neither side is the winner	Draw
Something through which one can see	Transparent
A man working only for money	Mercenary
A man walking on foot	Pedestrian
One who is all powerful	Omnipotent
One who has all knowledge	Omniscient
One who is present everywhere	Omnipresent
Naturally able to eat both animals and plants	Omnivorous
A thing which is out of place	Inopportune
An abnormality of temperament or character	Idiosyncrasy
A writer who steals the writings of another	Plagiarist
Repeating word for word	Verbatim
Medical examination of a dead body	Post-mortem
A medicine or drug used to prevent infection	Antiseptic
Talking to oneself all alone	Soliloquy
Notice of somebody's death	Obituary
Anything which is light and easy to carry	Portable
A period of growth between childhood and youth	Adolescence
To come to a foreign country as a settler	Immigrate
One who does things for pleasure	Amateur
One who is not able to pay his debts	Bankrupt

One Word

One who works for the welfare of women	Feminist
One who runs from justice	Fugitive
One who does not express himself freely	Introvert
One who helps needy people	Samaritan
A person who is indifferent to pain and pleasure	Stoic
One who loves books	Bibliophile
A statement which has more than one meaning	Ambiguous
A letter which does not bear the name or signature of the writer	Anonymous
Government by the people	Democracy
A person having same name as another	Namesake

MUST REMEMBER

➡ The key to good writing and speech often means to use less number of words to say the same number of things. 'One word' or shorter words help us replace worded expressions and phrases with just a single one.

PRACTICE EXERCISE

Choose the correct option to describe each of the following expressions.

1. One who looks on the bright side of things
   - (a) pessimist
   - (b) optimistic
   - (c) apprentice
   - (d) atheist

2. One who welcomes guests
   - (a) host
   - (b) guest
   - (c) invitee
   - (d) glutton

3. One who pretends to be what he is not
   - (a) cynic
   - (b) fanatic
   - (c) miser
   - (d) imposter

4. One who observes stars and other objects in space
   - (a) connoisseur
   - (b) astrologer
   - (c) astronomer
   - (d) martyr

5. A four-legged animal
   - (a) amphibian
   - (b) quadruped
   - (c) biped
   - (d) parasite

6. A man who loves mankind and works for the welfare of others
   - (a) philanthropist
   - (b) misanthropist
   - (c) plagiarist
   - (d) feminist

7. One who spends a lot
   - (a) miser
   - (b) mercenary
   - (c) spendthrift
   - (d) cosmopolitan

8. Repeating word for word
   - (a) epitaph
   - (b) verbatim
   - (c) oral
   - (d) linguist

9. A mark that cannot be removed
   - (a) incredible
   - (b) invisible
   - (c) invincible
   - (d) indelible

10. Food that cannot be eaten
    - (a) infallible
    - (b) indelible
    - (c) inedible
    - (d) insatiable

11. A man walking on foot
    - (a) pedestrian
    - (b) veteran
    - (c) refugee
    - (d) amateur

12. A notice of somebody's death
    - (a) soliloquy
    - (b) epitaph
    - (c) obituary
    - (d) post-mortem

13. Someone who cannot read or write
    - (a) stoic
    - (b) bibliophile
    - (c) amateur
    - (d) illiterate

14. Government by the people
    - (a) oligarchy
    - (b) aristocracy
    - (c) monocracy
    - (d) democracy

15. A speech delivered without preparation
    - (a) extempore
    - (b) verbatim
    - (c) soliloquy
    - (d) debate

16. A medicine or drug used to prevent infection
    - (a) tablet
    - (b) injection
    - (c) antiseptic
    - (d) vaccine

17. One who expresses himself freely
    - (a) introvert
    - (b) extrovert
    - (c) stoic
    - (d) eccentric

18. One who does not believe in god
    - (a) novice
    - (b) egotist
    - (c) monotheist
    - (d) atheist

19. One who eats human flesh
    - (a) carnivore
    - (b) herbivore
    - (c) omnivore
    - (d) cannibal

20. A work published after the author's death
    - (a) plagiarist
    - (b) posthumous
    - (c) anonymous
    - (d) epitaph

One Word

HOTS

Fill in the blanks with the most suitable word (one word) to complete the following sentences.

1. For a while, my uncle gambled every day, he could not stop himself. He became an _____.
   (a) addict   (b) connoisseur
   (c) adamant   (d) edict

2. My sister works with a reputed newspaper in London. She is a _____ by profession.
   (a) painter   (b) author
   (c) journalist   (d) singer

3. Annie has a huge collection of vinyl records, but the sad part is you cannot play them. The players are _____ now.
   (a) rare   (b) expensive
   (c) absolute   (d) obsolete

4. The bride was shocked to find out on her wedding day that the groom had _____ with his long-time lover.
   (a) eloped   (b) galloped
   (c) emailed   (d) eluded

5. The travel agent was yet to share the detailed _____ with the tourists the day before the departure.
   (a) items   (b) itinerary
   (c) tertiary   (d) seminary

6. Something inside of me kept telling me that things were going to go wrong today. I should have listened to the voice of my _____.
   (a) confidence   (b) clever
   (c) conscience   (d) mother

7. Although late for work, Ashish stopped his car to take the injured puppy to the clinic. He is the perfect example of a _____.
   (a) citizen   (b) Sumerian
   (c) Senorita   (d) Samaritan

8. The reason her health is deteriorating is because she cannot sleep at night. She suffers from some sort of _____.
   (a) insolvent   (b) insecure
   (c) insomnia   (d) insane

9. I have put in my best efforts to complete this project. However, I doubt Mrs. Johnson will like it. She is quite _____.
   (a) fascist   (b) tedious
   (c) fast   (d) fastidious

10. The ending of this novel is _____. The writer has left it on the readers to draw their own conclusions.
    (a) amphibious   (b) ambiguous
    (c) amorphous   (d) confusing

Phrasal Verbs and Idioms, Modals, Word Order

5

Learning Objectives : In this chapter, students will learn about:
- ✓ Some common Phrasal verbs
- ✓ Commonly used Idioms
- ✓ Uses of Modals
- ✓ Kinds of Word Order

CHAPTER SUMMARY

A phrasal verb consists of a verb and a participle. The participle can be a preposition or an adverb. Like idioms, the meaning of a phrasal verb cannot be arrived at by adding up the meaning of individual words.

Some commonly used phrases and their meanings are following.

Phrasal Verb	Meaning
Bear down	Overpower
Bear with	Tolerate
Bear out	Confirm
Bear up	Keep up spirits
Break through	Fail to keep
Break with	Cease to be friendly with
Call at	Visit
Call to	Address loudly
Call for	Demand for
Called on	Paid a brief visit
Take away	Remove
Taken to	Resorted to
Take after	Resemble
Take up with	Be friendly with
Take down	Record
Take in	Admit
Taken with	Pleased with
Struck dumb	Astonished
Struck off	Erased
Strike up	Begin to play
Stand against	Withstand
Stood up	Opposed
Set in	Begun
Set out	Started on
Set off	Depart
Set upon	Attacked
Set down	Record
Set forth	Explain
Draw up	Draft
Hear out	Listen until somebody has finished
Kept up	Maintained
Keep at	Continue doing
Keep from	Abstain from
Let loose	Set free
Let in	Allow to enter
Put in	Presented
Put out	Extinguish
Put down	Suppress

Put up with	Endure
Put off	Postponed
Brought about	Caused
Brought up	Reared
Bring out	Highlight
Brought out	Published
Come about	Happen
Come down	Descend
Come across	Meet accidently
Get away	Escape
Run down	Weak and tired
Held up	Detained
Cut out	Suitable
Pass off	Pretend to be
Blown up	Exaggerated
Die out	Disappear
Over and above	In addition to
Fall out	Had a quarrel
At home	Comfortably
Put across	To convey
Make away	Steal

Fall in	Agree
Work up	Excite
Taken aback	Surprised
Out and out	Thoroughly
Go over	Study carefully
Bowled over	Overwhelmed
Bear out	Support
Blow out	Extinguish
Catch up	Overtake
Drag on	Progress very slowly
Feel for	Search with the hands

Idioms

Idioms are a group of words used together to express something. The meaning of individual words gives little or no idea about the whole expression.

Example

'Blow your trumpet' is an idiom.

However, we cannot interpret its meaning as playing the musical instrument called trumpet. Used in an idiomatic sense, it means someone praising himself.

Commonly Used Idioms

S. No	Idiom	Meaning
1.	An arm and a leg	Very expensive
2.	Over the moon	Extremely pleased or happy
3.	Jumping the gun	Doing or starting something too early
4.	Once in a blue moon	Something that happens very rarely
5.	A chip on the shoulder	Feeling inferior or having a grievance about something
6.	A piece of cake	Very easy
7.	A drop in the ocean	A very small part of something much bigger
8.	A blessing in disguise	Something positive that isn't recognized until later
9.	Actions speak louder than words	It's better to actually do something rather than just talking about it
10.	It's a small world	Meeting someone you would not have expected to

11.	Back to the drawing board	When an attempt to do something fails and you have to start over again
12.	Caught between a rock and a hard place	Having two very bad choices
13.	Bite my tongue	Wanting to say something but stopping yourself.
14.	Cut to the chase	Leave out all the unnecessary details and just get to the point
15.	Putting all your eggs in one basket	Investing all of one's resources into one possibility
16.	Every cloud has a silver lining	Believing that every bad thing eventually leads to something good
17.	Found my feet	To become comfortable in what you are doing
18.	Got up on the wrong side of the bed	To mean that you are having a bad day
19.	Go an extra mile	Doing much more than is required when doing something
20.	Hit the nail on the head	Say exactly the right thing
21.	Heat of the moment	Saying or doing something suddenly without thinking about it
22.	Keep an eye on him	Watch someone or something carefully
23.	Kicked the bucket	Died
24.	Let sleeping dogs lie	Avoid a conflict
25.	Let the cat out of the bag	Tell someone something that you were not supposed to
26.	Don't bite the hand that feeds you	Hurt or upset someone who is helping you
27.	Sitting on the fence	Not making a firm decision between different choices
28.	Over the top	Excessive
29.	Practice makes a man perfet	Continuously doing something improves one's knowledge or skill.
30.	Pulling your leg	Joking around
31.	Take a rain check	To decline an offer that you will take up later
32.	As a rule of thumb	Principle that is strictly adhered to
33.	Smell a rat	To sense that something is not right
34.	Ball is in your court	Telling someone it's now their turn to make a decision
35.	Until the cows come home	For a very long time
36.	Tongue-in-cheek	Something said in humour rather than seriously
37.	Under the weather	Unwell
38.	Water under the bridge now	Things from the past that are not important anymore

39.	Judge a book by its cover	The belief that outside appearances do not reveal what someone or something is really like
40.	Working against the clock	Not having enough time to do something
41.	Flogging a dead horse	Attempting to continue with something that is over
42.	Bent over backwards	Doing all you can to help someone
43.	Break a leg	Good luck
44.	Hold your horses	Telling someone who is getting ahead of themselves to wait or be patient
45.	Driving someone up the wall	Annoying or irritating somebody

Modals

Modals are the helping verbs, which indicate the manner or mode of actions indicated by the main verb. They can be used to express obligation, permission, possibility, ability, etc. Modals are never used with other modals.

The most commonly used modals are:

Present Tense	Past Tense
can	could
may	might
shall	should
will	would
must	ought to

Uses of Modals

Modal verbs can be used in a variety of different forms.

- **Will** is used to make polite request and express future events.

  Example
  How long will this work take? (about a future event)
  Will you please close the door? (a polite request for doing something)

- **Shall** is used to show intention, threat, and for future events.

  Example
  I shall be there by 8:00 pm. (future event)
  Shall we move into the living room? (intention)
  He shall not escape me. (threat)

- **Would** is used to make a polite request.

  Example
  Would you please stop making noise? (polite request)

- **Should** is used to express necessity.

  Example
  We should do all we can to avoid war. (necessity)

- **Can** is used to indicate possibility and to give permission.

  Example
  I think I can get you a ticket to the concert. (possibility)
  You can come in now. (Permission)

- **Could** is used to show polite request.

  Example
  Could you tell me the time, please? (polite request)

- **May** is used to give and take permission.

  Example
  May I go now? (permission)
  Yes, you can leave now.

- **Must** is used to indicate necessity, compulsion or strong obligation.

  Example
  In order to pass, you must study for your exams. (necessity)
  They must pay the fine. (compulsion)
  You must be loyal to your country. (obligation)

Words Order

Words are arranged according to grammatical rules in a sentence. This arrangement or sequence of words is known as word order.

Kinds of Word Order

Normal Word Order
In most sentences the subject comes first, followed by the verb and then the object. We can call this the SVO order or the normal word order.

Example
Kelly baked a chocolate cake.
In this sentence **Kelly** is the subject, **baked** is the verb and **cake** is the object.

TRIVIA
Los Angeles' full name is "El Pueblo de Nuestra Senora la Reina de los Angeles de Porciuncula"

Inverted Word Order
Sometimes, in order to express an idea better, we deviate from the normal word order. In such sentences the subject comes after the verb or between verb parts.
This is known as inverted word order.

Example
A white castle sits up the hill. (SVO)
Up the hill sits a white castle. (Inverted word order)
In this sentence the subject 'white castle' follows the verb 'sits'.
I will never see her again. (SVO)
Never will I see her again. (Inverted word order)
Here, the subject 'I' is placed between the parts of verb 'will' and 'see'.

- A phrasal verb consists of a verb and a participle. The participle can be a preposition or an adverb.
- Idioms are a group of words used together to express something.
- Modals are the helping verbs, which indicate the manner or mode of actions indicated by the main verb.
- Modals are never used with other modals.
- In most sentences the subject comes first, followed by the verb and then the object.

PRACTICE EXERCISE

I. Fill in the blanks with the correct phrasal verb.

1. It's time to get rid of the old team and _____ in some fresh ideas.
   (a) set   (b) be
   (c) come   (d) bring

2. I'm very unhappy with the service and I intend to _____ in a complaint.
   (a) cave   (b) take
   (c) dig   (d) put

3. When we go to an art museum, it is usually to _____ the works of art.
   (a) look for   (b) look up
   (c) look after   (d) look at

4. I thought my English dictionary was lost, and I _____ it all over the house.
   (a) looked for   (b) looked at
   (c) looked after (d) look for

5. At the political demonstration the activists were busy _____ tracts against the government.
   (a) giving out   (b) giving up
   (c) gave out   (d) give out

6. When my younger daughter told me she was bored, I told her that she should _____ some sort of sport.
   (a) go in for   (b) go on
   (c) go round   (d) go out for

7. Whenever I want to stop doing these exercises, my teacher suggests that I _____ .
   (a) go on   (b) go over
   (c) go out   (d) go around

8. We were waiting for our new house, so we were glad that it _____ so fast.
   (a) went up   (b) go up
   (c) went into   (d) go on

9. My parents are taking me to New York for my next holidays; I am really _____ the trip.
   (a) look forward to
   (b) looking forward to
   (c) look forward
   (d) looked forward to

10. We need to _____ the price of the product, which is relatively high, and focus on its quality as a selling point.
    (a) back down   (b) break down
    (c) play down   (d) settle down

11. Have you _____ any other interesting product features that we could emphasize in the ads?
    (a) come across (b) drawn out
    (c) gotten across (d) made out

12. This poster is horrible and can't be used. The colors and images are all wrong. We will have to _____ .
    (a) do it over   (b) even it out
    (c) do it in   (d) put it down

13. We're going to have to _____ the advertising campaign if we can't get any TV or radio time.
    (a) call on   (b) call off
    (c) drop off   (d) drop out

14. I like that magazine, but I think we should _____ advertising in it until its circulation has increased.
    (a) put out   (b) put back
    (c) put away   (d) put off

15. My new assistant needs to be _____ before I trust her to run an ad campaign.
    (a) broken down (b) broken in
    (c) broken up   (d) broken into

16. He started to _____ when he reached the motorway.
    (a) speed off   (b) speed up
    (c) speed away   (d) none of these

17. You need to _____ a form to join the library.
    (a) fill on   (b) fill at
    (c) fill in   (d) none of these

18. The teacher told him to be quiet but he _____ talking.
    (a) Kept up   (b) Kept at
    (c) Kept on   (d) None of these

19. The alarm ___ at 6, but I didn't hear it.
    (a) went out   (b) went away
    (c) went off   (d) none of these

20. The fire was so big that the fire fighters had difficulties in _____ it _____ .
    (a) putting, off (b) putting, away
    (c) putting, out (d) none of these

II. **Choose the correct meaning of proverb/ idiom. If there is no correct meaning given, (e) 'None of these' will be the answer.**

1. To make clean breast of
   (a) To gain prominence
   (b) To praise oneself
   (c) To confess without of reserve
   (d) To destroy before it blooms
   (e) None of these

2. To keeps one's temper
   (a) To become hungry
   (b) To be in good mood
   (c) To preserve one's energy
   (d) To be aloof from
   (e) None of these

3. To catch a tartar
   (a) To trap wanted criminal with great difficulty
   (b) To catch a dangerous person
   (c) To meet with disaster
   (d) To deal with a person who is more than one's match
   (e) None of these

4. To drive home
   (a) To find one's roots
   (b) To return to place of rest
   (c) Back to original position
   (d) To emphasise
   (e) None of these

5. To have an axe to grind
   (a) A private end to serve
   (b) To fail to arouse interest
   (c) To have no result
   (d) To work for both sides
   (e) None of these

6. To cry wolf
   (a) To listen eagerly
   (b) To give false alarm
   (c) To turn pale
   (d) To keep off starvation
   (e) None of these

7. To end in smoke
   (a) To make completely understand
   (b) To ruin oneself
   (c) To excite great applause
   (d) To overcome someone
   (e) None of these

8. To be above board
   (a) To have a good height
   (b) To be honest in any business deal
   (c) They have no debts
   (d) To try to be beautiful
   (e) None of these

9. To put one's hand to plough
   (a) To take up agricultural farming
   (b) To take a difficult task
   (c) To get entangled into unnecessary things
   (d) Take interest in technical work
   (e) None of these

10. To pick holes
    (a) To find some reason to quarrel
    (b) To destroy something
    (c) To criticise someone
    (d) To cut some part of an item
    (e) None of these

11. To leave someone in the lurch
    (a) To come to compromise with someone
    (b) Constant source of annoyance to someone
    (c) To put someone at ease
    (d) To desert someone in his difficulties
    (e) None of these

12. To play second fiddle
    (a) To be happy, cheerful and healthy
    (b) To reduce importance of one's senior
    (c) To support the role and view of another person
    (d) To do back seat driving
    (e) None of these

13. To beg the question
    (a) To refer to
    (b) To take for granted
    (c) To raise objections
    (d) To be discussed
    (e) None of these

14. A black sheep
    (a) An unworthy person
    (b) A lucky person
    (c) An ugly person
    (d) A partner who takes no share of the profits
    (e) None of these

15. A man of straw
    (a) A man of no substance
    (b) A very active person
    (c) A worthy fellow
    (d) An unreasonable person
    (e) None of these

16. To smell a rat
    (a) To see signs of plague epidemic
    (b) To get bad small of a bad dead rat
    (c) To suspect foul dealings
    (d) To be in a bad mood
    (e) None of these

17. To hit the nail right on the head
    (a) To do the right thing
    (b) To destroy one's reputation
    (c) To announce one's fixed views
    (d) To teach someone a lesson
    (e) None of these

18. To set one's face against
    (a) To oppose with determination
    (b) To judge by appearance
    (c) To get out of difficulty
    (d) To look at one steadily
    (e) None of these

III. **Fill in the blanks with the correct option/ modal verb.**

1. _____ I borrow your book?
   (a) May   (b) Should
   (c) Would   (d) Will

2. You _____ to be present on the occasion.
   (a) will   (b) ought
   (c) must   (d) could

3. For this movie to be successful, everyone _____ play their parts well.
   (a) may   (b) could
   (c) would   (d) must

4. You _____ not have offended him.
   (a) will   (b) should
   (c) shall   (d) ought

5. If you don't hurry now, you _____ be late.
   (a) can   (b) cannot
   (c) ought   (d) will

6. _____ you like to have a drink?
   (a) May   (b) Should
   (c) Would   (d) Will

7. His version of the incident _____ be true.
   (a) may   (b) should
   (c) would   (d) will

8. It _____ rain soon.
   (a) ought   (b) can
   (c) may   (d) could

9. He _____ be friendly if he wants to.
   (a) ought   (b) can
   (c) may   (d) shall

10. I _____ be eighteen next month.
    (a) will   (b) can
    (c) may   (d) could

11. _____ I send for the doctor?
    (a) Ought   (b) Can
    (c) Might   (d) Shall

12. You _____ do what you are told.
    (a) ought   (b) can
    (c) must   (d) could

13. You _____ to pay your taxes as soon as possible.
    (a) ought   (b) can
    (c) may   (d) could

14. I _____ take care of everything for you.
    (a) may   (b) must
    (c) would   (d) shall

15. I _____ be swimming at the beach right now.
    (a) could   (b) may
    (c) will   (d) shall

16. Jessica's engagement ring is enormous. It _____ have cost a fortune.
    (a) may   (b) must
    (c) will   (d) shall

17. I _____ mail you my address.
    (a) may   (b) might
    (c) will   (d) ought

18. People _____ not tell a lie.
    (a) may   (b) must
    (c) will   (d) should

19. I _____ definitely be at the airport to receive you.
    (a) may   (b) must
    (c) will   (d) could

20. You _____ pay in cash. They do not accept credit cards.
    (a) may   (b) must
    (c) will   (d) shall

IV. **Choose the sentence which follows the correct word order.**

1. (a) She speaks English well.
   (b) She speaks well English.
   (c) She English well speaks.
   (d) She well speaks English.

2. (a) Sometimes I play tennis on Sundays.
   (b) Sometimes I tennis play on Sundays.
   (c) Sometimes I on Sundays play tennis.
   (d) I play sometimes tennis on Sundays.
3. (a) You're not supposed on the grass to walk.
   (b) To walk on the grass you're not supposed.
   (c) You're supposed not to walk on the grass
   (d) You're not supposed to walk on the grass.
4. (a) Every weekend she eats fish.
   (b) She eats fish every weekend.
   (c) Every weekend fish she eats.
   (d) Fish she eats every weekend.
5. (a) Do you often come here?
   (b) Often do you come here?
   (c) Do you come here often?
   (d) Come here do you often?
6. (a) He worked all week hard.
   (b) He worked hard all week.
   (c) Worked hard him all week.
   (d) He hard worked all week.
7. (a) Tell me where is she, could you?
   (b) Could you tell me she is where?
   (c) Could you tell me where is she?
   (d) Could you tell me where she is?
8. (a) I haven't spoken to her recently.
   (b) I haven't recently spoken to her.
   (c) Recently, I haven't to her spoken.
   (d) Recently spoken to her I haven't
9. (a) In a hurry I did my homework.
   (b) I did my homework in a hurry.
   (c) My homework in a hurry I did.
   (d) My homework I did in a hurry.
10. (a) They do not anymore live in Delhi.
    (b) They do not live in Delhi anymore.
    (c) In Delhi they do not live anymore.
    (d) Anymore in Delhi they do not live.
11. (a) Bonny sang yesterday very well.
    (b) Bonny very well sang yesterday.
    (c) Bonny sang very well yesterday.
    (d) Yesterday sang Bonny very well.
12. (a) Give it to me.
    (b) Give to me it.
    (c) Give me it.
    (d) Give it me.
13. (a) What I said you should tell him, under no circumstances.
    (b) You should tell him under no circumstances what I said.
    (c) Under no circumstances, you should tell him that I said.
    (d) Under no circumstances, should you tell him what I said.
14. (a) I saw a good film yesterday on TV.
    (b) On TV yesterday, I saw a good film.
    (c) I saw a good film on TV yesterday.
    (d) On TV yesterday, a good film I saw.
15. (a) As soon as I left the building, it started to rain.
    (b) As soon as I left the building, to rain it started.
    (c) As soon as the building I left, it started to rain.
    (d) The building I left as soon as it started to rain.
16. (a) Suddenly started crying the baby.
    (b) The baby suddenly started crying.
    (c) The baby started suddenly crying.
    (d) The baby started crying suddenly.
17. (a) Can you tell me what is the time?
    (b) Can you tell me what the time is?
    (c) What is the time, can you tell me?
    (d) What the time is, can you tell me?
18. (a) My computer works not.
    (b) Works not my computer.
    (c) My computer doesn't work.
    (d) My computer not works.
19. (a) We were for the show late.
    (b) Late we were for the show.
    (c) Late for the show we were.
    (d) We were late for the show.
20. (a) On the second floor is our flat.
    (b) On the second floor our flat is.
    (c) Our flat is on the second floor.
    (d) Our flat on the second floor is.

Phrasal Verbs and Idioms, Modals, Word Order

HOTS

I. Fill in the blanks with the correct phrasal verb.

1. If you wish to _____ with Pratap, you need to walk faster.
   (a) catch up (b) get up
   (c) cheer up (d) blow up

2. Several years after their fight, the two brothers finally _____.
   (a) made up (b) break up
   (c) dress up (d) hang up

3. I am not being able to _____ his intentions.
   (a) figure up (b) figure out
   (c) figure in (d) figure of

4. Sam and Clara's wedding has been ____ for a few days.
   (a) called off (b) given off
   (c) put off (d) set off

II. Fill in the blanks with the correct modal.

1. Varsha asked me when I _____ return her book.
   (a) should (b) will
   (c) must (d) can

2. _____ you teach me how to fix my computer?
   (a) Should (b) May
   (c) Will (d) Might

III. Choose the correct option for the given phrase.

1. Sit on the fence
   (a) to take the credit for something someone else did
   (b) when two (or more people) agree on something
   (c) when someone does not want to choose or make a decision
   (d) not to take what someone says too seriously

2. Don't put all your eggs in one basket
   (a) when something is done badly to save money
   (b) don't make plans for something that might not happen
   (c) do not put all your resources in one possibility
   (d) be optimistic, even difficult times bring something good in the end

IV. Choose the correct idiom and fill in the blanks.

1. I could have intervened when they were yelling at each other, but that would have just _____.
   (a) added fuel to the fire
   (b) cut corners
   (c) hit the sack
   (d) beat around the bush

2. The hired mourners at the funeral procession were only shedding _____.
   (a) barking up the wrong tree
   (b) whole nine yards
   (c) crocodile's tears
   (d) last straw

Nouns and Pronouns   6

Learning Objectives : In this chapter, students will learn about:
- ✓ Nouns and its types
- ✓ Pronouns and their types

CHAPTER SUMMARY

A noun is a naming word which expresses a person, a place, an animal, a thing, an idea or a feeling.
Examples: John, Jupiter, Singapore, elephant, book, teacher, man, girl, pencil, freedom, happiness.

Kinds of Noun

Proper Noun
Proper noun denotes a particular person, place or thing. They begin with capital letters.

Example
Barack Obama, China, Sunday, Titanic, The Himalayas, The Ganga are proper nouns.

Common Noun
Common noun is a common name given to every person or thing of same kind or class.

Example
Girl, doctor, animal, jaguar, flower, country, shop, month, ship.

Collective Noun
Collective noun refers to a collection of things spoken of as one whole.

Example
A flock of birds, a family, an audience, a herd of deer, an army.

Abstract Noun
Abstract noun refers to ideas, feelings, quality or concepts. We cannot see or touch these nouns.

Example
Love, beauty, courage, poverty, hunger.

Pronouns
Pronouns are used in place of nouns. They refer to the nouns mentioned previously. They are very useful to avoid repetition of nouns.

Example
Jessica's father asked <u>Jessica</u> to bring <u>Jessica's</u> father a pen.
(We can avoid repetition of the noun Jessica by using pronouns).
Jessica's father asked **her** to bring **him** a pen.
(In this sentence 'her' and 'him' are pronouns).

> **TRIVIA**
>
> Studies have shown that the average English native speaker knows about 20,000 words and with university-educated people knowing around 40,000 words.

Kinds of Pronoun

Personal Pronoun
Personal pronouns refer to the speaker, the person spoken to and the person spoken about. They are used when we do not want to mention the name of a person or thing more than once. Personal pronouns are: I, Me, You, It, We, Us, They, Them, He, Him, She, Her

Example
Parul is a close friend. Parul is from Delhi.
Parul is a close friend. **She** is from Delhi.

Sam loves staying in India. Sam does not want to leave.

Sam loves staying in India. **He** does not want to leave.

Possessive Pronoun

Possessive pronouns indicate possession or relationship of a person or thing to another person or thing. Possessive pronouns are: Mine, Yours, Hers, Ours, Theirs, His

Example

This book is **mine**. (Mine describes the relationship between the book and its owner).

I have lost my pen. May I use **yours**? (Yours indicates possession of the pen by a person).

Reflexive Pronoun

Reflexive pronoun is a special form of personal pronoun. It puts an emphasis on a person or thing.

Example

He **himself** said so.

I looked at **myself** in the mirror.

Relative Pronoun

Relative pronouns refer to the antecedent person or thing which they are used for in a sentence. Relative pronouns are: Who, Whose, Which, Whom, That

Example

The boy **who** is singing is my friend.

The car **which** I like is red.

The man **whom** I met yesterday is a magician.

Demonstrative Pronoun

Demonstrative pronouns point towards a particular thing or things. This, That, These, Those are demonstrative pronouns.

Example

This is my desk.

That is his choice.

These socks are mine.

Those are his shoes.

MUST REMEMBER

- A noun is a naming word which expresses a person, a place, an animal, a thing, an idea or a feeling.
- Proper noun denotes a particular person, place or thing. They begin with capital letters.
- Common noun is a common name given to every person or thing of same kind or class.
- Collective noun refers to a collection of things spoken of as one whole.
- Abstract noun refers to ideas, feelings, quality or concepts.
- Pronouns are used in place of nouns.
- Personal pronouns refer to the speaker, the person spoken to and the person spoken about.
- Possessive pronouns indicate possession or relationship of a person or thing to another person or thing.
- Reflexive pronoun is a special form of personal pronoun.
- Relative pronouns refer to the antecedent person or thing which they are used for in a sentence.
- Demonstrative pronouns point towards a particular thing or things. This, That, These, Those are demonstrative pronouns.

PRACTICE EXERCISE

I. Identify the type of underlined noun and choose the correct option.

1. Always speak the <u>truth</u>.
   (a) Proper   (b) Common
   (c) Collective   (d) Abstract
2. <u>Solomon</u> was the wisest of all kings.
   (a) Proper   (b) Common
   (c) Collective   (d) Abstract
3. <u>Cleanliness</u> is next to godliness.
   (a) Proper   (b) Common
   (c) Collective   (d) Abstract
4. The Nile is the longest of all <u>rivers.</u>
   (a) Proper   (b) Common
   (c) Collective   (d) Abstract
5. Jawaharlal Nehru was the first Prime Minister of <u>India.</u>
   (a) Proper   (b) Common
   (c) Collective   (d) Abstract
6. Birds of a feather <u>flock</u> together.
   (a) Proper   (b) Common
   (c) Collective   (d) Abstract
7. <u>Silver</u> and gold are precious metals.
   (a) Proper   (b) Common
   (c) Collective   (d) Abstract
8. <u>Man</u> pollutes his environment.
   (a) Proper   (b) Common
   (c) Collective   (d) Abstract
9. We were delayed because of the <u>traffic</u> jam.
   (a) Proper   (b) Common
   (c) Collective   (d) Abstract
10. It was <u>Edison</u> who invented the phonograph.
    (a) Proper   (b) Common
    (c) Collective   (d) Abstract

II. Choose the correct option to fill in the blanks with collective noun.

1. The competition will be judged by a _____ of experts.
   (a) panel   (b) gang
   (c) army   (d) crew
2. We can see a _____ of fish swimming in the crystal clear water.
   (a) pride   (b) team
   (c) litter   (d) shoal
3. Whenever there is a street fight, you will see a _____ of spectators gather around.
   (a) pack   (b) pair
   (c) crowd   (d) tribe
4. The _____ of dancers took the stage by storm with their performance.
   (a) troupe   (b) group
   (c) swarm   (d) troop
5. We saw a _____ of lions in the safari park.
   (a) chest   (b) pride
   (c) range   (d) flock
6. The children were tired after climbing up a _____ of stairs.
   (a) galaxy   (b) fleet
   (c) flight   (d) library
7. Marina dropped the _____ of rice before it reached the table.
   (a) stack   (b) piece
   (c) basket   (d) bowl
8. The children were happy to look after the _____ of puppies found in the park.
   (a) litter   (b) hive
   (c) flock   (d) catch
9. The thieves hid the loot in a _____ of hay.
   (a) bunch   (b) stack
   (c) bowl   (d) group
10. A _____ of ships sailed towards the harbor.
    (a) string   (b) flight
    (c) fleet   (d) herd

III. Choose the correct abstract noun for the given words. The first one is done for you.

1. Agent: _____
   (a) agency (correct answer)
   (b) agenda
   (c) agents
   (d) agentment
2. Act: _____
   (a) acting   (b) actor
   (c) actress   (d) action
3. Child: _____
   (a) parent   (b) childhood
   (c) playfulness   (d) kids

Nouns and Pronouns

4. Friend: _____
   (a) friends   (b) group
   (c) friendship   (d) school
5. Able: _____
   (a) disable   (b) ability
   (c) unable   (d) enable
6. Safe: _____
   (a) danger   (b) secure
   (c) unsafe   (d) safety
7. Strong: _____
   (a) weakness   (b) strength
   (c) powerful   (d) brave
8. Poor: _____
   (a) beggar   (b) rich
   (c) poverty   (d) hunger
9. Obey: _____
   (a) obedience   (b) disobey
   (c) obeying   (d) obeyed
10. Fly: _____
    (a) flying   (b) flight
    (c) flown   (d) flew

IV. Choose the correct option to identify the type of the underlined pronouns.

1. <u>Your</u> new bag looks expensive.
   (a) Personal   (b) Possessive
   (c) Reflexive   (d) Relative
2. <u>Our</u> favourite food is spaghetti.
   (a) Personal   (b) Possessive
   (c) Reflexive   (d) Relative
3. I had to remind <u>myself</u> to speak clearly and loudly.
   (a) Personal   (b) Possessive
   (c) Reflexive   (d) Relative
4. <u>Which</u> of you is going to the ceremony?
   (a) Personal   (b) Possessive
   (c) Reflexive   (d) Relative
5. Linda is my sister. <u>She</u> does not like sports.
   (a) Personal   (b) Possessive
   (c) Reflexive   (d) Relative
6. John blamed <u>himself</u> for the poor performance.
   (a) Personal   (b) Possessive
   (c) Reflexive   (d) Relative
7. She received many toys: two of <u>which</u> she gave to her sister.
   (a) Personal   (b) Possessive
   (c) Reflexive   (d) Relative
8. My mother's name is Anita. <u>She</u> is from India.
   (a) Personal   (b) Possessive
   (c) Reflexive   (d) Relative
9. I knew that <u>their</u> team was very disciplined.
   (a) Personal   (b) Possessive
   (c) Reflexive   (d) Relative
10. They thanked <u>themselves</u> for their luck.
    (a) Personal   (b) Possessive
    (c) Reflexive   (d) Relative

V. Fill in the blanks with the correct option.

1. Pedro and I like to play tennis. _____ play at the club.
   (a) We   (b) I
   (c) He   (d) Us
2. There are a lot of pets in our colony, but _____ is the most disciplined.
   (a) our   (b) ours
   (c) your   (d) their
3. Radhika's sincerity as a student made the teacher believe that _____ would never cheat.
   (a) his   (b) her
   (c) she   (d) him
4. At home my mother gives _____ cooking lessons.
   (a) I   (b) her
   (c) me   (d) mine
5. The women in blue saree is _____ mother.
   (a) my   (b) mine
   (c) ours   (d) theirs
6. He wanted to play the prank but _____ was afraid that he would be caught.
   (a) him   (b) his
   (c) he   (d) he's
7. Please put our name on the gift so that _____ know that it's from _____.
   (a) us/they   (b) they/us
   (c) them/they   (d) he/us
8. Our English teacher taught _____ Shakespeare this year.
   (a) our   (b) ours
   (c) us   (d) me

9. My parents will not allow _____ to spend the night outside.
   (a) me   (b) mine
   (c) I   (d) her

10. A papaya may not look tasty but _____ good for health.
    (a) it   (b) its
    (c) it's   (d) they

11. The story began to puzzle _____ when it did not make any sense.
    (a) they   (b) he
    (c) me   (d) she

12. My best friend wants me to stay with _____ tonight.
    (a) she   (b) hers
    (c) her   (d) she's

13. _____ house is located on a hill.
    (a) Ours   (b) Our
    (c) Theirs   (d) Who's

14. The baby started recognizing _____ in the mirror.
    (a) she   (b) her
    (c) herself   (d) it

15. We had to remind _____ that it's just a game.
    (a) us   (b) our
    (c) ours   (d) ourselves

16. Mom asked _____ to be careful not to spill the sauce.
    (a) I   (b) mine
    (c) me   (d) she

17. I intend to be at home immediately after the movie is over but _____ may be a little bit late.
    (a) me   (b) I
    (c) mine   (d) myself

18. He is not a good friend but he is an acquaintance of _____.
    (a) mine   (b) me
    (c) myself   (d) I

19. The gangster flashed _____ gun at us.
    (a) him   (b) his
    (c) himself   (d) his's

20. I took a picture of _____ with my new hat.
    (a) my   (b) me
    (c) mine   (d) myself

Nouns and Pronouns

HOTS

I. Choose the correct option to fill in the blanks with suitable noun. See the direction given in the brackets.

1. You broke my favourite _____. (common noun)
    (a) mug (b) snoopy mug
    (c) natraj (d) none of these

2. I really want to buy a new pair of _____. (proper noun)
    (a) jeans (b) Levis
    (c) clothes (d) none of these

3. They are all waiting for us at the _____. (common noun)
    (a) McDonalds (b) restaurant
    (c) dinner set (d) none of these

4. We are going for tomorrow's cricket match at the _____. (proper noun)
    (a) Eden Gardens (b) stadium
    (c) match (d) none of these

5. There are many patients waiting to see _____ at the clinic. (common noun)
    (a) Dr. verma (b) the doctor
    (c) patient (d) none of these

6. Rajeev drives a big _____ to work. (proper noun)
    (a) car (b) Honda City
    (c) bus (d) none of these

7. We were served _____ as soon as we entered the party. (common noun)
    (a) drinks (b) Coca Cola
    (c) food (d) none of these

8. The Titanic sank in the _____. (proper noun)
    (a) Atlantic (b) ocean
    (c) river (d) none of these

9. This time, we are planning a trip outside _____. (common noun)
    (a) India (b) the country
    (c) state (d) none of these

10. The Mona Lisa is one of the most popular paintings by _____. (proper noun)
    (a) Leonardo da Vinci (b) an artist
    (c) dentist (d) none of these

II. Fill in the blanks with correct pronoun.

1. _____ can help me?
    (a) Who (b) Which
    (c) Whom (d) Whose

2. With _____ did you play bad-minton yesterday?
    (a) who (b) whom
    (c) which (d) whose

3. We blamed _____ for our failure.
    (a) us (b) themselves
    (c) ourselves (d) myself

4. _____ books belong to her.
    (a) This (b) That
    (c) Them (d) These

5. The man laughed at <u>them</u>. Here the underlined word is an example of –
    (a) subject pronoun
    (b) reflexive pronoun
    (c) object pronoun
    (d) possessive pronoun

Verbs and Adverbs

Learning Objectives: In this chapter, students will learn about:
- Verbs and its types
- Basics of Adverbs
- Types of Adverbs

CHAPTER SUMMARY

Verbs show an action or a state of being.
Example
Drive, eat, sing, fall, give, read, bounce

Kinds of Verb
Verbs can be divided into three groups based on the use in a sentence.

Action Verb
Action verbs express an action (give, drink, walk). These verbs can be either transitive or intransitive. A **transitive verb** always has a noun that follows the action of the verb, called the direct object. An **intransitive verb** does not need an object to make the sense complete.

Example
Laura **raises** her hand.
('Raises' is the verb and 'hand' is the object, which is required to make the complete sense of the sentence.) Thus, 'Raises' is the transitive verb in this sentence.
He **swam** fast. ('Swam' is the verb. The word 'fast' modifies the verb, but there is no object required to make the sense complete.) Thus, 'swam' is an intransitive verb.

Verbs of Being
Verbs of being are not action words. These verbs express a state of existence. The most common of them are: 'am', 'are', 'is', 'was', and 'were'. They change form to agree with the subject.
Example
Lily **is** a student.

My father **was** away from the event.
Thus, the verbs – is, was – are showing the existence of the subject.

> **TRIVIA**
> English is the language of the air. This means that all pilots have to identify themselves and speak English while flying, regardless of their origin.

Auxiliary Verb
Auxiliary verbs are used before main verbs to show the time of the action. They are also known as helping verbs.

Example
Jasmine **will** drive to work tomorrow. In this sentence 'will' is the helping verb and 'drive' is the main verb.
Tejas **is going** to Australia. In this sentence 'is' is the helping verb and 'going' is the main verb.

> **Some auxiliary verbs are:**
> am, is, are, was, were, may, might, must, has, have, had, should, does, do, did, will, would, shall, can, could

Modal Verb
Modal verbs are used with other verbs to show obligation, permission, possibility, and other

Verbs and Adverbs

actions done. Modals are never used with other modals.

Example

How long **will** this work take?

(*In this sentence* 'will' *is used to state what we expect to happen. Thus, it is a modal verb.*)

I **will** be finishing these exercises by the time you return home.

(*In this sentence also* **will** *expresses future activity.*)

Other modal verbs and what they are used for:

Shall (intent), *would* (polite requests), *should/must* (obligation or necessity), *can* (possibility), *could* (ability) and *may* (permission).

Adverb

An adverb modifies a verb, an adjective or another adverb. Adverbs answer the questions 'when', 'where', 'how', 'why' and 'how much' or in 'what degree'.

Example

What are you writing on the paper?

Kinds of Adverb

Adverbs are classified according to their function in a sentence.

Adverbs are broadly divided into three classes – Simple, Interrogative and Relative.

Simple Adverbs

These adverbs are further divided into the following kinds of adverbs.

Adverbs of Time

These adverbs answer the question of 'when' an action took place.

Examples

We will go to a movie **tonight**.

She went shopping **yesterday**.

Sudha will be back from work **soon**.

Adverbs of Place

These adverbs answer the question of 'where' an action takes place.

Examples

I searched for my lost pen **everywhere**.

He went **downstairs** to the basement.

Adverbs of Frequency

These adverbs answer the question of 'how often' an action takes place.

Examples

Rohan practices the violin **regularly**.

My grandparents visit us **frequently**.

I go to the park **often**.

Adverbs of Manner

These adverbs answer the question of 'how' or 'in what manner' an action takes place.

Examples

Rohit speaks English **fluently**.

I was **terribly** upset with my brother.

The soldiers fought the war **bravely**.

Adverbs of Degree or Extent

These adverbs answer the question of 'how much' or 'in what degree' a quality is described or an action is performed. They precede the verb, adjective or other adverbs they describe.

Examples

Shikha is **least** interested in sports.

He was **slightly** feverish yesterday.

Her dress is **pretty** expensive.

The ceiling in this room is **fairly** high.

Manish **really** loves reading books.

He is **too** weak to walk.

Adverbs of Reason

These adverbs answer the question of 'why' an action takes place.

Examples

She didn't go to school **because** it was raining.

He did not study, **therefore** he failed his exams.

Sudha is ill, **hence** she will not come today.

Interrogative Adverbs

These adverbs are used to ask questions and are placed at the beginning of a sentence.

Examples

- **How** is your brother now?
- **Why** didn't she come last night?

Formation of Adverb

Adverb can be formed by adding 'ly' to nouns, verbs and adjectives.

Example

Sleep (verb)	Sleepily (adverb)
Clever (adjective)	Cleverly (adverb)
Day (noun)	Daily (adverb)
Noise (noun)	Noisily (adverb)

Adverb that do not end with 'ly' are called **irregular adverb**.

Example

Soon, often, yet, so, rather, around, never, fast.

- A transitive verb always has a noun that follows the action of the verb, called the direct object. An intransitive verb does not need an object to make the sense complete.
- Auxiliary verbs are used before main verbs to show the time of the action.
- Modal verbs are used with other verbs to show obligation, permission, possibility, and other actions done. Modals are never used with other modals.
- An adverb modifies a verb, an adjective or another adverb.
- Adverb can be formed by adding 'ly' to nouns, verbs and adjectives.
- Adverb that do not end with 'ly' are called irregular adverb.

PRACTICE EXERCISE

I. Fill in the blanks with correct form of action verb/option.

1. My sister _____ her homework late.
   (a) submitted (b) submit
   (c) submits (d) submitting

2. My younger brother _____ earlier in the night before his test.
   (a) sleep (b) slept
   (c) sleeping (d) sleeps

3. The teacher _____ us in all the remaining problems.
   (a) guide (b) guides
   (c) guided (d) guiding

4. The Moon _____ brightly at night.
   (a) shining (b) shiny
   (c) shine (d) shines

5. Manners _____ a man.
   (a) makes (b) make
   (c) made (d) making

6. My sister got me a _____ doll.
   (a) danced (b) dances
   (c) dance (d) dancing

7. _____ football is not just his hobby, but his profession.
   (a) Played (b) Play
   (c) Playing (d) Player

8. We _____ home from the picnic with the setting sun behind us.
   (a) returned (b) returning
   (c) return (d) returns

9. In order to _____ early in the morning, you must go to bed early.
   (a) wakes (b) wake
   (c) waking (d) awaken

10. We are encouraged _____ our teeth after every meal.
    (a) to brush (b) brush
    (c) brushing (d) brushed

11. I had a hard time staying _____ during the boring speech.
    (a) awoke (b) awake
    (c) awaken (d) awakened

12. I _____ to the park today.
    (a) to walk (b) walking
    (c) walk (d) walked

13. Peter _____ in China in 1965.
    (a) lived (b) lives
    (c) living (d) life

14. She goes _____ every morning.
    (a) run (b) running
    (c) ran (d) runs

15. My father _____ a newspaper every day.
    (a) buy (b) bought
    (c) buys (d) buying

II. Fill in the blanks with suitable verb of being.

1. They _____ visiting their grandmother next month.
   (a) are (b) is
   (c) am (d) was

2. I _____ looking for a way out of the maze.
   (a) are (b) is
   (c) am (d) was

3. Last evening, I _____ looking for my lost dog in the park.
   (a) are (b) is
   (c) am (d) was

4. The last time we met, you _____ shopping in the mall.
   (a) were (b) is
   (c) am (d) was

5. We _____ painting a house this weekend.
   (a) are (b) is
   (c) am (d) was

6. My brothers, Niki and Riki, _____ playing soccer this weekend.
   (a) are (b) is
   (c) am (d) was

7. Who _____ going to get the grocery this week?
   (a) are (b) is
   (c) am (d) were

8. It's hard to predict who will win but they _____ putting in their best effort.
   (a) are (b) is
   (c) am (d) was

9. I did not eat breakfast this morning, so I _____ getting a little hungry now.
   (a) are (b) is
   (c) am (d) was

10. Compared to my older brother, I _____ much shorter.
    (a) are	(b) is
    (c) am	(d) was
11. Rick was the only one without a project, as he _____ not listening in class yesterday.
    (a) are	(b) is
    (c) am	(d) was
12. The smell of garbage _____ awful.
    (a) are	(b) were
    (c) am	(d) was
13. I _____ doubtful about the outcome, so I am waiting eagerly.
    (a) are	(b) is
    (c) am	(d) was
14. Animals can become fierce if they _____ trapped.
    (a) are	(b) is
    (c) am	(d) was
15. What _____ you doing last year?
    (a) are	(b) is
    (c) am	(d) were

III. **Fill in the blanks with suitable auxiliary verb.**
1. What _____ you do every Sunday?
    (a) do	(b) are
    (c) have	(d) shall
2. I _____ explain the point to you.
    (a) can	(b) had
    (c) do	(d) have
3. She _____ not want to stay at home. She wants to go out with her friends.
    (a) do	(b) does
    (c) could	(d) should
4. What _____ you been doing?
    (a) have	(b) has
    (c) had	(d) could
5. I _____ be compelled to leave the room if you don't start behaving yourself.
    (a) should	(b) can
    (c) must	(d) shall
6. She _____ always wanted to meet him.
    (a) has	(b) are
    (c) have	(d) shall
7. If I were you, I _____ do it.
    (a) shouldn't	(b) didn't
    (c) can't	(d) wouldn't

8. That _____ have been a shooting star.
    (a) should	(b) would
    (c) must	(d) will
9. _____ I wait any longer?
    (a) Would	(b) Can
    (c) Should	(d) Could
10. I _____ run long distances when I was young.
    (a) has	(b) do
    (c) does	(d) had

IV. **Fill in the blanks with suitable adverb.**
1. I am a very punctual person. I am _____ late.
    (a) never	(b) usually
    (c) always	(d) frequently
2. Shirin's father is a dentist. He makes sure she _____ brushes her teeth before going to bed.
    (a) never	(b) always
    (c) sometimes	(d) rarely
3. Nathan had landed a dream job, his parents said _____.
    (a) sadly	(b) sinfully
    (c) slowly	(d) proudly
4. You look worn out. You have _____ been working too hard.
    (a) never	(b) quickly
    (c) probably	(d) comfortably
5. Although I am a vegetarian, my friends are _____ non-vegetarians.
    (a) always	(b) mostly
    (c) only	(d) humbly
6. I love watching Hindi films. But I also watch English films _____.
    (a) occasionally	(b) regularly
    (c) daily	(d) purely
7. Their behaviour seemed suspicious. _____ there is something wrong.
    (a) Highly	(b) Clearly
    (c) Sadly	(d) Dimly
8. I _____ I think I should take a long break.
    (a) never	(b) only
    (c) even	(d) sometimes
9. She is _____ the right person for the job.
    (a) angrily	(b) strongly
    (c) certainly	(d) carefully

Verbs and Adverbs

10. She got dressed _____ as soon as she heard her favourite singer was performing that day.
    (a) slowly   (b) quickly
    (c) rapidly   (d) cleverly
11. Unfortunately, our house is not big _____ for the party.
    (a) much   (b) too
    (c) enough   (d) soon
12. _____ many cooks spoil the broth.
    (a) Too   (b) To
    (c) Two   (d) Tow
13. He pushed the door _____.
    (a) patriotically (b) greatly
    (c) nicely   (d) forcefully
14. The kids shouted _____ as they played in the ground.
    (a) creatively   (b) cheerfully
    (c) cleverly   (d) foolishly
15. The turtle moved _____ and could not keep up with the rabbit.
    (a) daily   (b) firstly
    (c) quickly   (d) slowly

V. Fill in the blanks with suitable adverb that modifies the given word.

1. Whispered _____
   (a) softly   (b) loudly
   (c) forcefully   (d) really
2. Fell _____
   (a) appropriately   (b) accidentally
   (c) absolutely   (d) actively
3. Fought _____
   (a) barely   (b) brightly
   (c) busily   (d) bravely
4. Wounded _____
   (a) boldly   (b) cleanly
   (c) badly   (d) clearly
5. Listened _____
   (a) softly   (b) carefully
   (c) forcefully   (d) really
6. Shone _____
   (a) brightly   (b) currently
   (c) correctly   (d) chiefly
7. Smiled _____
   (a) simply   (b) safely
   (c) swiftly   (d) sweetly
8. Waited _____
   (a) perfectly   (b) physically
   (c) patiently   (d) painfully
9. Laughed _____
   (a) heartily   (b) lively
   (c) likely   (d) smiley
10. Studied _____
    (a) hungrily   (b) carefully
    (c) hugely   (d) hysterically

VI. Fill in the blanks with the correct adverbial form of the given words.

1. Create _____
   (a) creation   (b) creating
   (c) creatively   (d) creativity
2. Horror _____
   (a) horribly   (b) horrifying
   (c) horrible   (d) horrification
3. Lucky _____
   (a) luck   (b) luckily
   (c) luckless   (d) luckyly
4. Knowledge _____
   (a) know   (b) knowly
   (c) knowledgeable   (d) knowingly
5. Greed _____
   (a) greedily   (b) greediness
   (c) greedy   (d) greedful
6. Chaos _____
   (a) chaotic   (b) chaotically
   (c) chaosly   (d) chaosically
7. Frighten _____
   (a) fright   (b) fear
   (c) frighteningly   (d) frightful
8. Obey _____
   (a) obedience   (b) obediencely
   (c) obedient   (d) obediently
9. Loyal _____
   (a) loyalty   (b) loyally
   (c) loyalness   (d) loyalful
10. Tolerate _____
    (a) tolerance   (b) tolerable
    (c) tolerably   (d) toleration

HOTS

I. Fill in the blanks with the correct form of the verb.

1. Had I _____ his intentions, I _____ him.
   (a) know/would avoid
   (b) knew/avoid
   (c) known/would have avoided
   (d) none of these

2. He speaks as though he _____ a lawyer.
   (a) was   (b) is
   (c) been   (d) have

3. Whenever I go to that town, I _____ (make) it a point to visit the church there.
   (a) make   (b) made
   (c) have made   (d) had made

II. Fill in the blanks with the correct adverb.

1. He behaved so _____ that we were all shocked.
   (a) strange   (b) strangely
   (c) strangeness (d) stranger

2. Mayank visits his grandparents _____.
   (a) frequentness (b) frequent
   (c) frequency   (d) frequently

3. Is there a way to do it more _____?
   (a) easy   (b) easily
   (c) easiest   (d) easier

III. Read the following passage and select the options that can correctly replace the underlined portions.

1. The atmosphere of the class **Q1** different. My old teacher allowed us **Q2** if we had finished our work. The new teacher doesn't allow **Q3** at all. Our old teacher let us **Q4** our snacks in the classroom during break, but our new teacher has forbidden eating snacks in the classroom.
   (a) is now   (b) was now
   (c) Has been since (d) had been then

2. The atmosphere of the class **Q1** different. My old teacher allowed us **Q2** if we had finished our work. The new teacher doesn't allow **Q3** at all. Our old teacher let us **Q4** our snacks in the classroom during break, but our new teacher has forbidden eating snacks in the classroom.
   (a) talking   (b) to talk
   (c) Talked   (d) talk

3. The atmosphere of the class **Q1** different. My old teacher allowed us **Q2** if we had finished our work. The new teacher doesn't allow **Q3** at all. Our old teacher let us **Q4** our snacks in the classroom during break, but our new teacher has forbidden eating snacks in the classroom.
   (a) talked   (b) to talk
   (c) Talk   (d) talking

4. The atmosphere of the class **Q1** different. My old teacher allowed us **Q2** if we had finished our work. The new teacher doesn't allow **Q3** at all. Our old teacher let us **Q4** our snacks in the classroom during break, but our new teacher has forbidden eating snacks in the classroom.
   (a) eat   (b) ate
   (c) Eating   (d) to eat

Verbs and Adverbs

Adjectives

Learning Objectives : In this chapter, students will learn about:
- Kinds of adjectives
- Degree of Comparison

CHAPTER SUMMARY

Adjectives describe or modify nouns or pronouns. They identify or quantify another person or thing in a sentence. Adjectives usually preceed noun or pronoun that they modify.

Example
We were standing next to a **tall** tree.
It was a **cold** morning.
The **shortest** man won the race.
I am **happy** but they are **sad**.

Kinds of Adjective

Descriptive Adjective
Descriptive adjectives describe nouns. They tell us about the colour, size, shape, condition of a noun.

Example
Dangerous criminals, **green** vegetables, a **square** box, a **big** house, a **funny** story

Quantitative Adjective
Quantitative adjectives tell us the number (how many) or amount (how much) of a noun.

Example
He has eaten **three** apples.
I don't have **much** money.
A **little** learning is dangerous.

Demonstrative Adjective
Demonstrative adjectives are used to point out facts or indicate a particular noun or pronoun. 'This', 'that', 'these' and 'those' are demonstrative pronouns.

Example
This red balloon is mine.
That cute baby is his brother.
These two cats have stripes on their bodies.
I really like **those** shoes.

Possessive Adjective
Possessive adjectives express possession of a noun by someone or something.
'My', 'her', 'his', 'her', 'its', 'our' and 'their' are possessive adjectives.

Example
Her essay was considered the best.
This is **our** plan.

Degrees of Comparison
An adjective has three degrees of comparison. These degrees are positive, comparative and superlative.

Positive Degree
The positive degree simply describes a noun or a pronoun.

Example
Sharon is a **tall** girl.
Debbie is a **clever** girl.
An adjective may also be used to make comparison between two equal things or persons.

Example
Sharon is as **clever** as Debbie.
Debbie is as **tall** as Sharon.

Comparative Degree
The comparative degree is used to compare two unequal persons or things.

Example
Brinda is **clever** than Alisha.

Suman is **taller** than Sudha.
This box is heavier than that.

Superlative Degree
The superlative degree is used to compare three or more persons or things of unequal quality.

Example
Indra is the **tallest** among his brothers.
Carl Lewis is the **fastest** runner in the world.

TRIVIA

The word with the maximum number of definitions in English is 'Set' with amazingly around 464 definitions.

Formation of Degrees of Comparison

Rule1: Most adjectives form the comparative degree by adding 'er' and the superlative degree by adding 'est' to the positive degrees.

Positive	Comparative	Superlative
Bright	Brighter	Brightest
Black	Blacker	Blackest
Bold	Bolder	Boldest
Clever	Cleverer	Cleverest
Cold	Colder	Coldest
Fast	Faster	Fastest
Great	Greater	Greatest

Positive	Comparative	Superlative
High	Higher	Highest
Kind	Kinder	Kindest
Small	Smaller	Smallest
Strong	Stronger	Strongest
Sweet	Sweeter	Sweetest
Tall	Taller	Tallest
Young	Younger	Youngest

Rule 2: For adjectives ending with 'e', the comparative is formed by adding only 'r' and the superlative by adding only 'st' to the positive degree.

Example

Positive	Comparative	Superlative
Brave	Braver	Bravest
Fine	Finer	Finest
Large	Larger	Largest
Noble	Nobler	Noblest
Pale	Paler	Palest
Simple	Simpler	Simplest
Wise	Wiser	Wisest
White	Whiter	Whitest

Rule 3: If an adjective ends with 'y', the comparative is formed by deleting the 'y' by adding 'ier' and the superlative is formed by replacing the final 'y' with 'iest'.

Positive	Comparative	Superlative
Costly	Costlier	Costliest
Dry	Drier	Driest
Easy	Easier	Easiest
Happy	Happier	Happiest
Healthy	Healthier	Healthiest
Heavy	Heavier	Heaviest
Lazy	Lazier	Laziest
Merry	Merrier	Merriest

Rule 4: The comparative and superlative is formed by doubling the final consonant and then adding 'er' and 'est' respectively to the positive degree.

Positive	Comparative	Superlative
Big	Bigger	Biggest
Fat	Fatter	Fattest
Hot	Hotter	Hottest
Thin	Thinner	Thinnest
Dim	Dimmer	Dimmest

Adjectives

Rule 5: Adjectives with more than one syllable form comparative and superlative by just adding 'more' and 'most' respectively with positive form.

Positive	Comparative	Superlative
Active	More active	Most active
Attractive	More attractive	Most attractive
Beautiful	More beautiful	Most beautiful
Brilliant	More brilliant	Most brilliant
Careful	More careful	Most careful
Courageous	More courageous	Most courageous
Cunning	More cunning	Most cunning
Difficult	More difficult	Most difficult
Famous	More famous	Most famous
Popular	More popular	Most popular

Rule 6: There are some irregular comparisons in which the comparative and superlative are different words.

Positive	Comparative	Superlative
Bad	Worse	Worst
Good	Better	Best
Little	Less	Least
Much	More	Most
Many	More	Most
Far	Farther	Farthest

MUST REMEMBER

- Adjectives describe or modify nouns or pronouns. Adjectives usually preceed noun or pronoun that they modify.
- Descriptive adjectives describe nouns. They tell us about the colour, size, shape, condition of a noun.
- Quantitative adjectives tell us the number (how many) or amount (how much) of a noun.
- Demonstrative adjectives are used to point out facts or indicate a particular noun or pronoun.
- Possessive adjectives express possession of a noun by someone or something.
- The superlative degree is used to compare three or more persons or things of unequal quality.

PRACTICE EXERCISE

I. Fill in the blanks with suitable adjective.

1. Make sure you wear a scarf because the weather outside is quite _____.
   (a) windy (b) humid
   (c) hot   (d) rainy

2. My new bed not only looks good but is also very _____.
   (a) heavy   (b) ugly
   (c) comfortable (d) stiff

3. The little _____ kitten climbed up the curtains and spilled her milk.
   (a) naughty (b) lazy
   (c) old   (d) fat

4. We sat and watched as the setting sun created a _____ sky
   (a) dull   (b) clear
   (c) gorgeous (d) dark

5. I will be performing in front of a large audience tomorrow, so I am feeling _____.
   (a) angry   (b) anxious
   (c) jealous (d) sleepy

6. The younger sister felt _____ as the elder one was being showered with presents on her birthday.
   (a) foolish (b) wise
   (c) jealous (d) poor

7. Helping my mother with the chores seemed fun at first, but soon it became _____.
   (a) relaxed   (b) tedious
   (c) exciting (d) happening

8. She is too _____ to learn the error of her ways.
   (a) arrogant   (b) hardworking
   (c) disciplined (d) wise

9. She was _____ to receive the bad news.
   (a) happy   (b) excited
   (c) shocked (d) elated

10. It was so _____ of you to offer them help.
    (a) rude (b) horrible
    (c) kind (d) terrible

II. Fill in the blanks with the correct form of adjective.

1. Of his three sisters, Susan is the _____.
   (a) old   (b) elder
   (c) eldest (d) None of these

2. Very few books are read _____ Harry Potter by children.
   (a) as much as (b) more than
   (c) most   (d) None of these

3. Black is the _____ colour.
   (a) dark   (b) darker
   (c) darkest (d) None of these

4. Maya is the _____ girl in the class.
   (a) pretty   (b) prettier
   (c) prettiest (d) None of these

5. Tina is _____ than Priti.
   (a) intelligent   (b) more intelligent
   (c) most intelligent (d) None of these

6. The weather today is _____ than the weather yesterday, but not as _____ as it was four days ago.
   (a) worse/bad   (b) bad/bad
   (c) worse/worse (d) None of these

7. The road was _____ than we expected.
   (a) long   (b) longer
   (c) longest (d) None of these

8. Planes are the _____ means of travelling today.
   (a) convenient   (b) more convenient
   (c) most convenient (d) None of these

9. These jeans are the _____, in fact they are _____ than the trousers.
   (a) dirty/dirtier   (b) dirtiest/dirtier
   (c) dirty/dirty   (d) None of these

10. A candle gives _____ light than a lamp.
    (a) little (b) less
    (c) least   (d) None of these

11. That boy is the _____ runner of all.
    (a) fast   (b) faster
    (c) fastest (d) None of these

12. His badminton skills are me _____, among the players in the team.
    (a) good (b) better
    (c) best (d) None of these

13. The cake is just as _____ as the ice-cream.
    (a) sweet   (b) sweeter
    (c) sweetest   (d) None of these

Adjectives

14. Shakespeare is _____ than any other English poet.
    (a) great (b) greater
    (c) greatest (d) None of these
15. Shakespeare is the _____ of all English poets.
    (a) great (b) greater
    (c) greatest (d) None of these
16. The pen is _____ than the sword.
    (a) mighty (b) mightier
    (c) mightiest (d) None of these
17. Mount Everest is the _____ peak in the world.
    (a) high (b) higher
    (c) highest (d) None of these
18. Mango is _____ than lime.
    (a) sweet (b) sweeter
    (c) sweetest (d) None of these
19. I have _____ books than you.
    (a) many (b) more
    (c) most (d) None of these
20. Very few nations are as _____ as the USA.
    (a) powerful (b) more powerful
    (c) most powerful (d) None of these

HOTS

Read the following passage and select options that can correctly replace the underlined portions.

1. Malaysia is **Q1** country and is blessed with plenty of rain and sunshine. Many types of trees and plants grow here. These trees bear **Q2** fruits. The 'King of Fruits' is without doubt the durian. It is **Q3** fruit. It has **Q4** skin. Inside, however, the fruit is **Q5**. It has a strong smell. The locals love the durian, but foreigners find the smell hard to bear.
    (a) a tropical, developing, small
    (b) a developing, tropical, small
    (c) A small, tropical, developing
    (d) A small, developing, tropical

2. Malaysia is **Q1** country and is blessed with plenty of rain and sunshine. Many types of trees and plants grow here. These trees bear **Q2** fruits. The 'King of Fruits' is without doubt the durian. It is **Q3** fruit. It has **Q4** skin. Inside, however, the fruit is **Q5**. It has a strong smell. The locals love the durian, but foreigners find the smell hard to bear.
    (a) delicious, sweet, many
    (b) Delicious, many, sweet
    (c) Many, delicious, sweet
    (d) Sweet, delicious, many

3. Malaysia is **Q1** country and is blessed with plenty of rain and sunshine. Many types of trees and plants grow here. These trees bear **Q2** fruits. The 'King of Fruits' is without doubt the durian. It is **Q3** fruit. It has **Q4** skin. Inside, however, the fruit is **Q5**. It has a strong smell. The locals love the durian, but foreigners find the smell hard to bear.
    (a) big, oval-shaped, a
    (b) An oval-shaped, big
    (c) A big, oval-shaped
    (d) The oval-shaped, big

4. Malaysia is **Q1** country and is blessed with plenty of rain and sunshine. Many types of trees and plants grow here. These trees bear **Q2** fruits. The 'King of Fruits' is without doubt the durian. It is **Q3** fruit. It has **Q4** skin. Inside, however, the fruit is **Q5**. It has a strong smell. The locals love the durian, but foreigners find the smell hard to bear.
    (a) a thorny, green or yellow
    (b) A green or yellow, thorny
    (c) Thorny, a green or yellow
    (d) Green or yellow, a thorny

5. Malaysia is **Q1** country and is blessed with plenty of rain and sunshine. Many types of trees and plants grow here. These trees bear **Q2** fruits. The 'King of Fruits' is without doubt the durian. It is **Q3** fruit. It has **Q4** skin. Inside, however, the fruit is **Q5**. It has a strong smell. The locals love the durian, but foreigners find the smell hard to bear.
    (a) soft, sweet, yellow
    (b) Sweet, soft, yellow
    (c) Sweet, yellow, soft
    (d) Yellow, soft and sweet

Articles and Prepositions

Learning Objectives : In this chapter, students will learn about:
- ✓ Different articles and their usage
- ✓ Concept of Preposition

CHAPTER SUMMARY

An article is used with a noun to indicate the type of reference being made by the noun. Articles specify grammatical definiteness of the noun, in some languages extending to volume or numerical scope. Articles are used before nouns.

Example

The earth revolves round *the* sun. Radha eats *an* orange.

Kinds of Articles

Articles are of two kinds: indefinite and definite.

Indefinite Article

The words 'a' and 'an' are indefinite articles. They are used before singular nouns that are countable.

☞ 'A' is used with the words that begin with a consonant sound.

Example

a book, a cat, a picture, a table, a lawyer

☞ 'A' is also used before the words (even if not a consonant) that begin with a 'u' sound. It is used before the word 'one' as well, although it begins with the vowel 'o', because it is pronounced 'wun'.

Example

a European country, a university, a uniform, a one-man army, a one-day seminar

☞ 'An' is used with words that begin with a vowel.

Example

an elephant, an owl, an apple, an item

☞ 'An' is also used before words that have a silent 'h' (not pronounced).

Example

An hour, an honest person

Definite Article

The word 'the' is the definite article. It is used before particular or definite persons or objects. It is used before all the things that one-of-a-kind.

Example

The best doctor, the favourite student, the sweetest fruit

Uses of Definite Article

We use the definite article in front of a noun when we believe the reader or listener knows exactly what we are referring to.

☞ When there is only one or unique thing

Example

The moon is very bright tonight.

Ramesh is the tallest boy in the class.

☞ Because there is only one in that place or in those surroundings:

Example

We live in a small village next to the church. = (the church in our village)

Look at the boy in the blue shirt over there. = (the boy I am pointing at)

☞ Because we have already mentioned it:

Example

A woman who fell 10 metres from High Peak was lifted to safety by a helicopter. The woman fell while climbing.

☞ We also use the definite article:
(i) To say something about all the things referred to by a noun:
Example
The heart pumps blood around the body. (= Hearts pump blood around bodies)
(ii) We use the definite article to talk about musical instruments:
Example
She is learning the guitar. (= She is learning to play any guitar)
(iii) To refer to a system or service:
How long does it take on the train?
You should tell the police.
(iv) With **adjectives** like rich, poor, elderly, unemployed to talk about **groups of people**:
Example
I think **the rich** should pay more taxes.

Omission of Article

We do not normally use the definite article with names:
Example
Paris is the capital of France.
But we do use the definite article with:
(i) **Countries** whose names include words like *kingdom, states* or *republic*:
Example
The United Kingdom; The Kingdom of Nepal; The United States
(ii) **Countries** which have **plural nouns** as their names:
Example
The Netherlands; The Philippines
(iii) **Geographical features**, such as mountain ranges, groups of islands, rivers, seas, oceans and canals:
Example
The Himalayas; The Canaries; The Atlantic Ocean; The Panama Canal.
(iv) **Newspapers**:
Example
The Times of India
(v) well known **buildings** or **works of art**:
Example
The Taj Mahal; The Mona Lisa

(vi) **Organisations**:
Example
The United Nations
(vii) **Hotels, pubs** and **restaurants**:
Example
the Ritz Hotel; the King's Head
(viii) **Families**:
Example
The Obamas; The Clintons

TRIVIA
In English, One of the oldest, shortest, most commonly used words in old and modern English is "I".

Prepositions

A word or a group of words such as in, from, to, out of and on behalf of, used before a noun or pronoun to show place, position, time or method is called a preposition.

Prepositions show the relationship between a noun or a pronoun and the remaining words in a sentence.

Example
He waited for me **at** the crossing.
We are **against** child labour.
The cat went and hid **under** the table.

Types of Prepositions

There are mainly of five types of prepositions:
- Preposition of Place
- Preposition of Time
- Preposition of Direction
- Preposition of Movement
- Preposition of Position

☞ **Preposition of Place:** There are three prepositions of places.
- **At** is used for a point of place (for small towns, villages or less important or small places)
  Examples
  At home
  At the exit/entrance

At work

He lives at Meharauli in Delhi.

- **In** is used for spaces, for large places, countries, large towns, state of rest or position inside anything.

    Examples

    He lives in Delhi.

    He is in his room.

    He lives at Panji in Goa.

- **On** is used for surface tops

    Examples

    We sat on the ground.

    The book is lying on the table.

    Rama is on the way

    He is working on the computer

☞ **Preposition of Time:** There are two prepositions of Time.

- **At** is used to indicate precise time.

    Examples

    At ten o'clock

    He came at sunset

    At this moment…

    He will start at 5 pm.

- **In** is used to indicate a period of time.

    Examples

    Amitabh Bachchan was born in 1942.

    He was born in Ireland in the eighteenth century.

☞ **Preposition of Direction:** There are eight prepositions of direction.

- **To** is used to indicate a specific destination

    Example

    I am going to my office.

- **Towards** is used to refer to direction of the destination.

    Examples

    I am going towards the station. [It means I am not going to the station but in the same direction.]

- **From** is used for the point of departure.

    Example

    He has come from the club.

- **Off** is used to indicate either *'being taken away from'* or *'down from'* i.e. when two things separate.

    Examples

    The cat fell off the tin roof.

    The aeroplane took off at 4 pm.

- **Against** is means *'pressing against'* i.e. used to indicate contact or pressure

    Example

    The motorcycle leaned against the wall.

- **For** is used to indicate direction only when the verb indicates the beginning of a movement.

    Example

    He is leaving for London today.

- **Out of** is used to indicate departure from a place/location

    Example

    John went out of the classroom.

- **At** is used when we want to say *'face to face with'*

    Examples

    I was looking at the photograph.

    I was sitting at the table.

☞ **Preposition of Movement:** There are six prepositions of movement.

- **Into** refers to the movement towards the interior.

    Example

    He jumped into the river.

- **Through/Across** is used to show the movement from one side to the other

    Examples

    He swam across the river.

    The hunters went through the forest.

- **Onto** is used to show the movement on an object.

    Example

    The ball rolled onto the pavement.

- **Along** is used to show the movement that is 'adjacent in line' or say 'in the same line'

    Example

    He walked along the bank of river.

- **In/On/By** is used to indicate a means of something.

Articles and Prepositions

Example

He came <u>by</u> foot.

- **Up/Down** is used to show the movement across an upper or lower level

    Example

    Jack and Jill climb <u>up</u> the hill.

☞ **Preposition of Position:** There are six prepositions of position.

- **Between** is used when we refer to persons.

    Example

    What happened <u>between</u> these two I do not know.

- **Among** is used when we refer to more than two persons.

    Example

    <u>Among</u> all the five brothers he is the best.

- **Over/Above:** Above means 'higher than' but over means 'vertically above'

    Examples

    They stay <u>above</u> the shop.

    The ceiling fan is <u>over</u> the table.

- **Below, Under:** Below means 'lower than' whereas under means 'vertically below'

    Examples

    I saw him standing <u>below</u> the building.

    The cat went <u>under</u> the floor.

    Exception: He is sitting <u>in</u> the shade of the tree. [Not under the shade.]

- **Beneath:** It means 'lower position/layer/level', but generally it is used figuratively.

    Example

    We sat <u>beneath</u> the apple tree.

- **Underneath:** It means 'directly below' something facing towards ground.

    Example

    The tunnel goes right <u>underneath</u> the city.

MUST REMEMBER

→ An article is used with a noun to indicate the type of reference being made by the noun.

→ The words 'a' and 'an' are indefinite articles. They are used before singular nouns that are countable.

→ The word 'the' is the definite article. It is used before particular or definite persons or objects.

→ We use the definite article in front of a noun when we believe the reader or listener knows exactly what we are referring to.

→ A word or a group of words such as in, from, to, out of and on behalf of, used before a noun or pronoun to show place, position, time or method is called a preposition.

→ Prepositions show the relationship between a noun or a pronoun and the remaining words in a sentence.

PRACTICE EXERCISE

I. Fill in the blanks with the correct article. Write 'None' where no article is required.

1. India is one of _____ largest countries in the world.
    (a) the   (b) a
    (c) an   (d) none

2. I never watch _____ television.
    (a) the   (b) a
    (c) an   (d) none

3. In fact, I haven't got _____ television.
    (a) the   (b) a
    (c) an   (d) none

4. _____ Taj Mahal is _____ popular tourist attraction.
    (a) The/a   (b) A/a
    (c) The/the   (d) None/the

5. _____ New Delhi is _____ capital of India.
    (a) The/the   (b) none/the
    (c) none/a   (d) none

6. They went for _____ walk around _____ park nearby.
    (a) the/a   (b) a/the
    (c) a/an   (d) the/none

7. _____ hotel where they held their wedding reception was called _____ Grand Hotel.
    (a) The/a   (b) The/the
    (c) A/a   (d) None/the

8. Ananya was born in _____ India, but she lives in _____ USA now.
    (a) the/the   (b) none/none
    (c) an/the   (d) none/the

9. My father's favourite newspaper is _____ Times of India.
    (a) the   (b) a
    (c) an   (d) none

10. He went on _____ expensive holiday to _____ Andamans.
    (a) The/the   (b) a/the
    (c) an/the   (d) none/none

11. _____ Gateway of India is in _____ Mumbai.
    (a) The/the   (b) A/the
    (c) The/none   (d) None/the

12. Which is _____ highest mountain in _____ world?
    (a) the/the   (b) a/the
    (c) an/the   (d) none/the

13. We had _____ very nice meal. _____ eggs were specially good.
    (a) the/The   (b) a/An
    (c) a/The   (d) none/An

14. New York is _____ exciting city, full of _____ adventures.
    (a) a/an   (b) an/an
    (c) an/none   (d) none/an

15. The company I work with has _____ offices all over India.
    (a) the   (b) a
    (c) an   (d) none

16. I have two brothers: one of them is still in _____ college and the other one has _____ graduated.
    (a) the/none   (b) a/none
    (c) a/a   (d) none/none

17. He told me that he met _____ alien once from _____ outer space.
    (a) the/an   (b) an/an
    (c) an/the   (d) none/an

18. That's _____ hard story to believe.
    (a) the   (b) a
    (c) an   (d) none

19. My uncle, _____ elderly man is _____ honest person.
    (a) an/a   (b) a/a
    (c) an/an   (d) none/none

20. He once saved _____ one-year-old boy from _____ fire.
    (a) a/none   (b) a/the
    (c) an/the   (d) none/the

21. Look at _____ apples on that tree. They are so large.
    (a) the   (b) a
    (c) an   (d) none

22. _____ life would be very difficult without _____ electricity.
    (a) none/the   (b) none/a
    (c) none/an   (d) none/none

Articles and Prepositions

23. Are you interested in _____ art or _____ architecture?
    (a) a/none   (b) none/a
    (c) none/none   (d) an/an
24. _____ violence is never justified.
    (a) the   (b) a
    (c) an   (d) none
25. I would love to live near _____ sea.
    (a) the   (b) a
    (c) an   (d) none

II. **Fill in the blanks with the correct preposition.**

1. The cat fell _____ the well.
   (a) above   (b) into
   (c) on   (d) in
2. The policeman walked _____ his jeep.
   (a) at   (b) too
   (c) towards   (d) by
3. Will you drop me _____ the airport tomorrow morning.
   (a) in   (b) to
   (c) at   (d) on
4. We will be in Kolkata _____ Christmas.
   (a) in   (b) during
   (c) at   (d) along
5. The author wrote the book _____ five weeks.
   (a) of   (b) off
   (c) on   (d) in
6. They have been friends _____ school days.
   (a) till   (b) onto
   (c) into   (d) since
7. The children played in the park _____ it grew dark.
   (a) till   (b) still
   (c) towards   (d) beyond
8. My mother and aunt talk to each other on the phone _____ hours.
   (a) off   (b) on
   (c) in   (d) for
9. My younger brother was born _____ New Delhi.
   (a) in   (b) on
   (c) by   (d) for
10. I have been working ever _____ I passed out of college.
    (a) after   (b) since
    (c) before   (d) until
11. Mother would not let me go out _____ I finished cleaning my room.
    (a) still   (b) without
    (c) until   (d) upon
12. During winter, the temperature drops _____ zero degrees in several places in North India.
    (a) down   (b) by
    (c) above   (d) below
13. I asked him _____ stop talking or leave.
    (a) to   (b) by
    (c) for   (d) in
14. There is no direct flight _____ India and the USA.
    (a) from   (b) between
    (c) to   (d) for
15. There is no direct flight _____ India to the USA.
    (a) for   (b) to
    (c) between   (d) from
16. Next month, I will be travelling _____ a few days.
    (a) for   (b) by
    (c) in   (d) on
17. It was too torrentially raining _____ go out.
    (a) for   (b) to
    (c) but   (d) onto
18. In the last year, the Yamuna water rose _____ the danger mark during monsoons.
    (a) beyond   (b) below
    (c) above   (d) until
19. The thief jumped _____ the wall and fled.
    (a) on   (b) over
    (c) in   (d) under
20. I hope to complete this project _____ next week.
    (a) to   (b) for
    (c) by   (d) since
21. The traffic was too dense to drive _____.
    (a) by   (b) away
    (c) through   (d) after

22. We are having a meeting _____ Monday to discuss safety issues in our block.
    (a) in   (b) by
    (c) on   (d) for
23. My brother got married _____ London.
    (a) in   (b) on
    (c) during   (d) into
24. We are going to see my parents _____ the weekend.
    (a) by   (b) under
    (c) over   (d) across
25. I have been waiting for you _____ 7 o'clock.
    (a) until   (b) till
    (c) for   (d) since
26. I don't like walking alone in the streets _____ night.
27. What are you doing _____ Saturday?
    (a) at   (b) in
    (c) on   (d) by
28. We are going to Delhi _____ train.
    (a) by   (b) in
    (c) on   (d) for
29. We moved _____ our new house last week.
    (a) beyond   (b) onto
    (c) into   (d) along
30. The little boy fell _____ the ground.
    (a) onto   (b) into
    (c) in   (d) on

(a) on   (b) in
(c) at   (d) by

HOTS

Fill in the blanks with suitable preposition.

1. We must be kind _____ strangers.
   (a) to   (b) for
   (c) from   (d) on
2. _____ of being fined, he was sent to prison.
   (a) to   (b) instead
   (c) from   (d) on
3. I apologized Akash _____ my rudeness _____ him.
   (a) to, for   (b) for, towards
   (c) from, on   (d) on, to
4. In scientific experiments _____ accuracy is essential and John could not judge _____ accuracy of the calculations.
   (a) an, the
   (b) no article, an
   (c) no article, the
   (d) no article, no article
5. Water is necessary for _____ life but _____ life of these insects does not depend on water.
   (a) no article, no article
   (b) no article the
   (c) the, the
   (d) a, the

Conjunctions and Punctuations 10

Learning Objectives : In this chapter, students will learn about:
- Conjunctions and its different types
- Different Punctuations

CHAPTER SUMMARY

A conjunction joins words, phrases or sentences together. Conjunctions are linking words and play a very important role in construction of sentences.

Example
'and', 'but', 'or'.

Kinds of Conjunctions
There are mainly two types of conjunction: coordinating conjunctions and subordinating conjunctions.

Coordinating Conjunction
Coordinating conjunctions join two thoughts (words or phrases) that are equally important in a sentence. The two thoughts they join are complete and can exist on their own as well.

There are seven coordinating conjunctions: For, And, Nor, But, Or, Yet, So.

Uses of Coordinating Conjunctions
- **For** explains reason or purpose

    Example
    I go to the park every Sunday for I like to take a long walk.

- **And** adds one thing to another

    Example
    I like to go to the park every Sunday and take a long walk.

- **Nor** presents an alternative

    Example
    I don't like to go to the park nor do I like walking.

- **But** establishes contrast

    Example
    I like to go to the park but I hate walking.

- **Or** gives a choice

    Example
    I stay at home on Sunday evenings or I go to the park.

- **Yet** contrasts one idea with another, which follow each other logically

    Example
    I always take a book to the park, yet I never read.

- **So** shows effect or consequence

    Example
    I have bought new running shoes, so I have to go to the park.

Subordinating Conjunction
Subordinating conjunctions are used to join two thoughts (words or phrases) where one of the thoughts is dependent on the other for meaning or relevance.

The dependent thought cannot exist on its own in a sentence.

Example
Since the boys misbehaved, they were punished.

She left early *because* her parents called her.

Wait here *until* I return.

Before the school reopens, we must finish our holiday homework.

Once you are at home, have a chat with your sister.
As soon as the cake is baked, we shall have it.
Commonly used subordinating conjunctions are:

after	although	as	as soon as
because	before	by the time	even if
even though	if	in case	rather than
since	so that	though	until
when	whenever	where	whereas
wherever	whether	while	how

Correlative Conjunction

Correlative conjunctions are a pair of conjunctions that are always used together.

Uses of Correlative Conjunctions

☞ **Both/and**

Example

She won gold medals from *both* single *and* group races.

☞ **Either/or**

Example

I am fine with *either* Monday *or* Wednesday.

☞ **Neither/nor**

Example

Neither you *nor* I will get off early today.

☞ **Not only/but also**

Example

Not only red *but also* green looks good on you.

TRIVIA

We can pronounce 'ough' in English in nine different ways. The sentence contains all forms of 'ough' : A rough-coated, dough-faced, thoughtful ploughman strode through the streets of scarborough; after falling into a slough, he coughed and hiccoughed.

Punctuation

Punctuation marks are symbols that are used to aid the clarity and comprehension of written language. Some common punctuation marks are the period, comma, question mark, and hyphen.

Period (.)

The period is also known as a full stop because it signals a speaker or reader that the sentence has come to an end.

Examples

The dog is brown.
My sister's name is Reeta.
The baby is crying.

Uses of Period

Rule 1: We use a period at the end of sentences that are statements.
A statement is a sentence that states, or tells, something.
Examples
I like to eat pizza.
The school starts on Wednesday.
The baby's name is Munna.

Rule 2: We use a period at the end of sentences that are commands.
A command is a sentence that tells someone to do something.
Examples
Pick up the blue ball.
Turn left at the next light.
Hand me the pencil.

Rule 3: We use a period at the end of sentences that are indirect questions.
An indirect question is a question that is said as a statement. It uses a period instead of a question mark.
Examples
She asked me why I didn't go to school yesterday.
I wondered why Bob wasn't there.
Suresh asked about that book.

Rule 4: We use period in abbreviations.
An abbreviation is a shortened version of a word or words.
Examples
United States of America is abbreviated as U.S.A.
Mr. is the abbreviation for Mister.
Rd. is the abbreviation for road.

Rule 5: We use period in website addresses.
Examples
www.dictionary.com
www.learnersdictionary.com
www.really-learn-english.com

Conjunctions and Punctuations

Omission of Period

Rule 1: Do not put a space before a period used to end a sentence.

Examples

The shirt is blue. (Correct)

The shirt is blue . (Incorrect)

Rule 2: Do put one space after the period if it is followed by another sentence.

Examples

I am driving to the city. The city is north of here. (Correct)

I am driving to the city.　The city is north of here. (Incorrect)

Importance of Period

Rule 1: If you do not use a period at the end of a sentence, each sentence will run into the next. That would create confusion for the speaker or reader. The period signals the end of a thought.

Example

I visited my friend in the city she lives with her mom they rent an apartment on the south side of town we had a nice visit I hope I can return next year. (Example without periods)

I visited my friend in the city. She lives with her mom. They rent an apartment on the south side of town. We had a nice visit. I hope I can return next year. (Example with periods)

Rule 2: Abbreviations without periods would be random letters placed together without making a word. The period or periods in an abbreviation signal to the reader that it is a shortened form of a word or words.

Rule 3: Websites will not work without periods. You must place a period in all correct places for the internet addresses to be correct.

Comma

Commas are the most frequently used punctuation marks. Commas customarily indicate a brief pause; they're not as final as periods.

Uses of Comma

Rule 1: Use commas to separate words and word groups in a simple series of three or more items.

Example

My property goes to my husband, son, daughter-in-law, and nephew.

Note: When the last comma in a series comes before and or or (after daughter-in-law in the above example), it is known as the Oxford comma. Most newspapers and magazines drop the Oxford comma in a simple series, apparently feeling it's unnecessary. However, omission of the Oxford comma can sometimes lead to misunderstandings.

Example

We had coffee, cheese and crackers and grapes.

Adding a comma after crackers makes it clear that cheese and crackers represents one dish. In cases like this, clarity demands the Oxford comma.

Example

We had coffee, cheese and crackers, and grapes.

Fiction and non-fiction books generally prefer the Oxford comma. Writers must decide Oxford or no Oxford and not switch back and forth, except when omitting the Oxford comma could cause confusion as in the cheese and crackers example.

Rule 2: Use a comma to separate two adjectives when the order of the adjectives is interchangeable.

Example

He is a strong, healthy man. (We could also say healthy, strong man.)

We stayed at an expensive summer resort. (We would not say summer expensive resort, so no comma.)

Another way to determine if a comma is needed is to mentally put and between the two adjectives. If the result still makes sense, add the comma. In the examples above, a strong and healthy man makes sense, but an expensive and summer resort does not.

Rule 3a: Many inexperienced writers run two independent clauses together by using a comma instead of a period. This results in the dreaded run-on sentence or, more technically, a comma splice.

Example

He walked all the way home, he shut the door. (Incorrect)

There are several simple remedies:

He walked all the way home. He shut the door. (Correct)

After he walked all the way home, he shut the door. (Correct)

He walked all the way home, and he shut the door. (Correct)

Rule 3b: In sentences where two independent clauses are joined by connectors such as and, or, but, etc., put a comma at the end of the first clause.

Example

He walked all the way home and he shut the door. (Incorrect)

He walked all the way home, and he shut the door. (Correct)

Some writers omit the comma if both the clauses are quite short:

Example

I paint and he writes.

Rule 3c: If the subject does not appear in front of the second verb, a comma is generally unnecessary.

Example

He thought quickly but still did not answer correctly.

But sometimes a comma in this situation is necessary to avoid confusion.

I saw that she was busy and prepared to leave. (Confusing)

I saw that she was busy, and prepared to leave. (Clearer with comma)

Without a comma, the reader is liable to think that 'she' was the one who was prepared to leave.

Rule 4a: When starting a sentence with a dependent clause, use a comma after it.

Example

If you are not sure about this, let me know now.

Follow the same policy with introductory phrases.

Example

Having finally arrived in town, we went shopping.

However, if the introductory phrase is clear and brief (three or four words), the comma is optional.

Example

When in town we go shopping.

But always add a comma if it would avoid confusion.

Example

On last Sunday, evening classes were cancelled. (The comma prevents a misreading.)

When an introductory phrase begins with a preposition, a comma may not be necessary even if the phrase contains more than three or four words.

Example

Into the sparkling crystal ball he gazed.

If such a phrase contains a series of prepositions, a comma may be used unless a verb immediately follows the phrase.

Examples

Between your house on Main Street and my house on Grand Avenue, the mayor's mansion stands proudly.

Between your house on Main Street and my house on Grand Avenue is the mayor's mansion.

However, if the introductory phrase contains more than one preposition, use a comma.

Example

With thanks to you, I accept this award.

Rule 4b: A comma is usually unnecessary when the sentence starts with an independent clause followed by a dependent clause.

Example

Let me know now if you are not sure about this.

Rule 5: Use commas to set off non-essential words, clauses, and phrases.

Example

Ginni who is my sister shut the door. (Incorrect)

Ginni, who is my sister, shut the door. (Correct)

The man knowing it was late hurried home. (Incorrect)

The man, knowing it was late, hurried home. (Correct)

In the preceding examples, note the comma after sister and late. Non-essential words, clauses, and phrases that occur midsentence must be enclosed by commas. The closing comma is called an appositive comma. Many writers forget to add this important comma. Following are two instances of the need for an appositive comma with one or more nouns.

Example

My best friend, Shankar arrived. (Incorrect)

My best friend, Shankar, arrived. (Correct)

The three items, a book, a pen, and paper were on the table. (Incorrect)

The three items, a book, a pen, and paper, were on the table. (Correct)

Rule 6: If something or someone is sufficiently identified, the description that follows is considered non-essential and should be surrounded by commas.

Example
Manohar, who has a limp, was in an auto accident. (If we already know which Manohar is meant, the description is not essential.)
The boy who has a limp was in an auto accident. (We do not know which boy is meant without further description; therefore, no commas are used.)
This leads to a persistent problem. Look at the following sentence:
Example
My brother Sumit is here.
Now, see how adding two commas changes the meaning:
Example
My brother, Sumit, is here.
Careful writers and readers understand that the first sentence means I have more than one brother. The commas in the second sentence mean that Sumit is my only brother.
Why? In the first sentence, Sumit is essential information: it identifies which of my two (or more) brothers I'm speaking of. This is why no commas enclose Sumit.
In the second sentence, Sumit is non-essential information—whom else but Sumit could I mean?—hence the commas.
Comma misuse is nothing to take lightly. It can lead to a train wreck like this:
Example
Mark Twain's book, Tom Sawyer, is a delight. (Because of the commas, that sentence states that Twain wrote only one book. In fact, he wrote more than two dozen of them.)
Rule 7a: Use a comma after certain words that introduce a sentence such as well, yes, why, hello, hey.
Examples
Why, I can't believe this!
No, you can't have a dollar.
Rule 7b: Use commas to set off expressions that interrupt the sentence flow (nevertheless, after all, by the way, on the other hand, however).
Example
I am, by the way, very nervous about this.
Rule 8: Use commas to set off the name, nickname, term of endearment, or title of a person directly addressed.
Examples

Will you, Aisha, do that assignment for me?
Yes, old friend, I will.
Good day, Captain.
Rule 9: Use a comma to separate the day of the month from the year, and—what most people forget!—always put one after the year, also.
Example
It was in the Sun's June 5, 2003, edition.
No comma is necessary for just the month and year.
Example
It was in a June 2003 article.
Rule 10: Use a comma to separate a city from its state, and remember to put one after the state, also.
Example
I'm from the Akron, Ohio, area.
Rule 11: Traditionally, if a person's name is followed by Sr. or Jr., a comma follows the last name: Martin Luther King, Jr. This comma is no longer considered mandatory. However, if a comma does precede Sr. or Jr., another comma must follow the entire name when it appears midsentence.
Example
Raman Sr. is here. (Correct)
Raman, Sr., is here. (Correct)
Raman, Sr. is here. (Incorrect)
Rule 12: Similarly, use commas to enclose degrees or titles used with names.
Example
Raman M.D., is here.
Rule 13a: Use commas to introduce or interrupt direct quotations.
Examples
He said, "I don't care."
"Why," I asked, "don't you care?"
This rule is optional with one-word quotations.
Example
He said 'Stop.'
Rule 13b: If the quotation comes before he said, she wrote, they reported, Dana insisted, or a similar attribution, end the quoted material with a comma, even if it is only one word.
Examples
"I don't care," he said.
"Stop," he said.

Rule 13c: If a quotation functions as a subject or object in a sentence, it might not need a comma.
Examples
Is "I don't care" all you can say to me?
Saying "Stop the car" was a mistake.

Rule 13d: If a quoted question ends in midsentence, the question mark replaces a comma.
Example
"Will you still be my friend?" she asked.

Rule 14: Use a comma to separate a statement from a question.
Example
I can go, can't I?

Rule 15: Use a comma to separate contrasting parts of a sentence.
Example
That is my money, not yours.

Rule 16a: Use a comma before and after certain introductory words or terms such as namely, that is, i.e., e.g., and for instance, when they are followed by a series of items.
Example
You may be required to bring many items, e.g., sleeping bags, pans, and warm clothing.

Rule 16b: A comma should precede the term etc. Many authorities also recommend a comma after etc. when it is placed midsentence.
Example
Sleeping bags, pans, warm clothing, etc., are in the tent.

> **Note:** The abbreviation i.e. means 'that is'; e.g. means 'for example.'

Semicolon

It's no accident that a semicolon is a period atop a comma. Like commas, semicolons indicate an audible pause—slightly longer than a comma's, but short of a period's full stop.

Semicolons have other functions too. But first, a caveat: avoid the common mistake of using a semicolon to replace a colon.

Examples
I have one goal; to find her. (Incorrect)
I have one goal: to find her. (Correct)

Rule 1a: A semicolon can replace a period if the writer wishes to narrow the gap between two closely linked sentences.

Examples
Call me tomorrow; you can give me an answer then.
We have paid our dues; we expect all the privileges listed in the contract.

Rule 1b: Avoid a semicolon when a dependent clause comes before an independent clause.
Examples
Although they tried; they failed. (Incorrect)
Although they tried, they failed. (Correct)

Rule 2: Use a semicolon before such words and terms as namely, however, therefore, that is, i.e., for example, for instance, when they introduce a complete sentence. It is also preferable to use a comma after these words and terms.
Example
Bring any two items; however, sleeping bags and tents are in short supply.

Rule 3: Use a semicolon to separate units of a series when one or more of the units contain commas.
Examples
The conference has people who have come from Moscow, Idaho, Springfield, California, Alamo, Tennessee, and other places as well. (Incorrect) (Note that with only commas, that sentence is hopeless.)
The conference has people who have come from Moscow, Idaho; Springfield, California; Alamo, Tennessee; and other places as well. (Correct) (Note the final semicolon, rather than a comma, after Tennessee.)

Rule 4: A semicolon may be used between independent clauses joined by a connector, such as and, but, or, nor, when one or more commas appear in the first clause.
Example
When I finish here, and I will soon, I'll be glad to help you; and that is a promise I will keep.

Rule 5: Do not capitalize ordinary words after a semicolon.
Example
I am here; You are over there. (Incorrect)
I am here; you are over there. (Correct)

Colon

A colon means "that is to say" or "here's what I mean." Colons and semicolons should never be used interchangeably.

Rule 1a: Use a colon to introduce a series of items. Do not capitalize the first item after the colon (unless it's a proper noun).

Examples

You may be required to bring many things: sleeping bags, pans, utensils, and warm clothing.

I want the following items: butter, sugar, and flour.

I need an assistant who can do the following: input data, write reports, and complete tax forms.

Rule 1b: A capital letter generally does not introduce a word, phrase, or incomplete sentence following a colon.

Examples

He got what he worked for: a promotion

He got what he worked for: a promotion that paid a higher wage.

Rule 2: Avoid using a colon before a list when it directly follows a verb or preposition that would ordinarily need no punctuation in that sentence.

Examples

I want: butter, sugar, and flour. (Not recommended)

I want butter, sugar, and flour. (Recommended) or Here is what I want: butter, sugar, and flour.

I've seen the greats, including: Barrymore, Guinness, and Streep. (Not recommended)

I've seen the greats, including Barrymore, Guinness, and Streep. (Recommended)

Rule 3: When listing items one by one, one per line, following a colon, capitalization and ending punctuation are optional when using single words or phrases preceded by letters, numbers, or bullet points. If each point is a complete sentence, capitalize the first word and end the sentence with appropriate ending punctuation. Otherwise, there are no hard and fast rules, except be consistent.

Examples

I want an assistant who can do the following:
- input data
- write reports
- complete tax forms

The following are requested:
- wool sweaters for possible cold weather.
- wet suits for snorkeling.
- introductions to the local dignitaries.

These are the pool rules:
- Do not run.
- If you see unsafe behavior, report it to the lifeguard.
- Did you remember your towel?
- Have fun!

Rule 4: A colon instead of a semicolon may be used between independent clauses when the second sentence explains, illustrates, paraphrases, or expands on the first sentence.

Example

He got what he worked for: he really earned that promotion.

If a complete sentence follows a colon, as in the previous example, authorities are divided over whether to capitalize the first word. Some writers and editors feel that capitalizing a complete sentence after a colon is always advisable. Others advise against it. Still others regard it as a judgment call: If what follows the colon is closely related to what precedes it, there is no need for a capital. But if what follows is a general or formal statement, many writers and editors capitalize the first word.

Example

Remember the old saying: Be careful what you wish for.

Rule 5: Capitalize the first word of a complete or full-sentence quotation that follows a colon.

Example

The host made an announcement: "You are all staying for dinner."

Rule 6: Capitalize the first word after a colon if the information following the colon requires two or more complete sentences.

Example

Dad gave us these rules to live by: Work hard. Be honest. Always show up on time.

Rule 7: If a quotation contains two or more sentences, many writers and editors introduce it with a colon rather than a comma.

Example

Dad often said to me: "Work hard. Be honest. Always show up on time."

Rule 8: For extended quotations introduced by a colon, some style manuals say to indent one-half inch on both the left and right margins; others say to indent only on the left margin. Quotation marks are not used.

Example

The author of Touched, Jane Straus, wrote in the first chapter:

Georgia went back to her bed and stared at the intricate patterns of burned moth wings in the translucent glass of the overhead light. Her father was in "hyper mode" again where nothing could calm him down.

Rule 9: Use a colon rather than a comma to follow the salutation in a business letter, even when addressing someone by his or her first name. (Never use a semicolon after a salutation.) A comma is used after the salutation in more informal correspondence.

Examples
Dear Ms. Rodriguez:
Dear Dave,

Question Mark

Rule 1: Use a question mark only after a direct question.

Example
Will you go with me? (Correct)
I'm asking if you will go with me? (Incorrect)

Rule 2a: A question mark replaces a period at the end of a sentence.

Example
Will you go with me? (Incorrect)

Rule 2b: Because of Rule 2a, capitalize the word that follows a question mark.

Some writers choose to overlook this rule in special cases.

Example
Will you go with me? with Joe? with anyone?

Rule 3a: Avoid the common trap of using question marks with indirect questions, which are statements that contain questions. Use a period after an indirect question.

Example
I wonder if he would go with me? (Incorrect)
I wonder if he would go with me. (Correct) **OR** I wonder: Would he go with me?

Rule 3b: Some sentences are statements—or demands—in the form of a question. They are called rhetorical questions because they don't require or expect an answer. Many should be written without question marks.

Examples
Why don't you take a break.
Would our kids knock it off.
What wouldn't I do for you!

Rule 4: Use a question mark when a sentence is half statement and half question.

Example
You do care, don't you?

Rule 5a: The placement of question marks with quotation marks follows logic. If a question is within the quoted material, a question mark should be placed inside the quotation marks.

Examples
She asked, "Will you still be my friend?"
The question Will you still be my friend? is a part of the quotation.
Do you agree with the saying, "All's fair in love and war"?
The question Do you agree with the saying? is outside the quotation.

Rule 5b: If a quoted question ends in mid sentence, the question mark replaces a comma.

Example
"Will you still be my friend?" she asked.

Parentheses and Brackets

Parentheses and brackets must never be used interchangeably.

Parentheses

Rule 1: Use parentheses to enclose information that clarifies or is used as aside.

Example
He finally answered (after taking five minutes to think) that he did not understand the question.

If material in parentheses ends a sentence, the period goes after the parentheses.

Example
He gave me a nice bonus ($500).

Commas could have been used in the first example; a colon could have been used in the second example. The use of parentheses indicates that the writer considered the information less important—almost an afterthought.

Rule 2a: Periods go inside parentheses only if an entire sentence is inside the parentheses.

Example
Please read the analysis. (You'll be amazed.)

This is a rule with a lot of wiggle room. An entire sentence in parentheses is often acceptable without an enclosed period:

Example
Please read the analysis (you'll be amazed).

Rule 2b: Take care to punctuate correctly when punctuation is required both inside and outside parentheses.

Example
You are late (aren't you?).

Note the question mark within the parentheses. The period after the parentheses is necessary to bring the entire sentence to a close.

Rule 3: Parentheses, despite appearances, are not part of the subject.

Example
John (and his trusty mutt) was always welcome.

If this seems awkward, try rewriting the sentence:

Example
John (accompanied by his trusty mutt) was always welcome.

Rule 4: Commas are more likely to follow parentheses than precede them.

Example
When he got home, (it was already dark outside) he fixed dinner. (Incorrect)

When he got home (it was already dark outside), he fixed dinner. (Correct)

Brackets

Brackets are far less common than parentheses, and they are only used in special cases. Brackets (like single quotation marks) are used exclusively within quoted material.

Rule 1: Brackets are interruptions. When we see them, we know they've been added by someone else. They are used to explain or comment on the quotation.

Example
"Four score and seven [today we'd say eighty-seven] years ago..."
"Bill shook hands with [his son] Al."

Rule 2: When quoting something that has a spelling or grammar mistake or presents material in a confusing way, insert the term sic in italics and enclose it in nonitalic (unless the surrounding text is italic) brackets.

Sic ("thus" in Latin) is shorthand for, "This is exactly what the original material says."

Example
She wrote, "I would rather die then [sic] be seen wearing the same outfit as my sister." (The [sic] indicates that then was mistakenly used instead of than.)

Rule 3: In formal writing, brackets are often used to maintain the integrity of both a quotation and the sentences others use it in.

Example
"[T]he better angels of our nature" gave a powerful ending to Lincoln's first inaugural address. (Lincoln's memorable phrase came midsentence, so the word the was not originally capitalized.)

Apostrophe

Rule 1a: Use the apostrophe to show possession. To show possession with a singular noun, add an apostrophe plus the letter s.

Example
a woman's hat
the boss's wife
Mrs. Chang's house

Rule 1b: Many common nouns end in the letter 's' (lens, cactus, bus, etc.). So do a lot of proper nouns (Mr. Jones, Texas, Christmas). There are conflicting policies and theories about how to show possession when writing such nouns. There is no right answer; the best advice is to choose a formula and stay consistent.

Rule 1c: Some writers and editors add only an apostrophe to all nouns ending in s. And some add an apostrophe + s to every proper noun, be it Hastings's or Jones's.

One method, common in newspapers and magazines, is to add an apostrophe + s ('s) to common nouns ending in s, but only a stand-alone apostrophe to proper nouns ending in s.

Example
The class's hours
Mr. Jones' golf clubs
The canvas's size
Texas' weather

Care must be taken to place the apostrophe outside the word in question. For instance, if talking about a pen belonging to Mr. Hastings, many people would wrongly write Mr. Hasting's pen (his name is not Mr. Hasting).

Example

Mr. Hastings' pen (Correct)

Another widely used technique is to write the word as we would speak it. For example, since most people saying "Mr. Hastings' pen" would not pronounce an added s, we would write Mr. Hastings' pen with no added s. But most people would pronounce an added s in "Jones's," so we'd write it as we say it: Mr. Jones's golf clubs. This method explains the punctuation of for goodness' sake.

Rule 2a: Regular nouns are nouns that form their plurals by adding either the letter s or -es (guy, guys; letter, letters; actress, actresses; etc.). To show plural possession, simply put an apostrophe after the s.

Example

Guys' night out (guy + s + apostrophe) (Correct)
Guy's night out (implies only one guy) (Incorrect)
Two actresses' roles (actress + es + apostrophe) (Correct)
Two actress's roles (Incorrect)

Rule 2b: Do not use an apostrophe + s to make a regular noun plural.

Example

Apostrophe's are confusing. (Incorrect)
Apostrophes are confusing. (Correct)
We've had many happy Christmas's. (Incorrect)
We've had many happy Christmases. (Correct)

In special cases, such as when forming a plural of a word that is not normally a noun, some writers add an apostrophe for clarity.

Example

Here are some do's and don'ts.

In that sentence, the verb do is used as a plural noun, and the apostrophe was added because the writer felt that dos was confusing. Not all writers agree; some see no problem with dos and don'ts. However, with single lowercase letters, it is advisable to use apostrophes.

Example

My a's look like u's.

Imagine the confusion if you wrote that sentence without apostrophes. Readers would see as and us, and feel lost.

Rule 2c: English also has many irregular nouns (child, nucleus, tooth, etc.). These nouns become plural by changing their spelling, sometimes becoming quite different words. You may find it helpful to write out the entire irregular plural noun before adding an apostrophe or an apostrophe + s.

Example

Two childrens' hats (Incorrect) (The plural is children, not childrens.)
Two children's hats (children + apostrophe + s) (Correct)
The teeths' roots (Incorrect)
The teeth's roots (Correct)

Rule 2d: Things can get really confusing with the possessive plurals of proper names ending in s, such as Hastings and Jones.

If you're the guest of the Ford family — the Fords — you're the Fords' guest (Ford + s + apostrophe). But what if it's the Hastings family?

Most would call them the "Hastings." But that would refer to a family named "Hasting." If someone's name ends in s, we must add -es for the plural. The plural of Hastings is Hastingses. The members of the Jones family are the Joneses.

To show possession, add an apostrophe.

Example

The Hastings' dog (Incorrect)
The Hastingses' dog (Hastings + es + apostrophe) (Correct)
The Jones' car (Incorrect)
The Joneses' car (Correct)

In serious writing, this rule must be followed no matter how strange or awkward the results.

Rule 2e: Never use an apostrophe to make a name plural.

Example

The Wilson's are here. (Incorrect)
The Wilsons are here. (Correct)
We visited the Sanchez's. (Incorrect)
We visited the Sanchezes. (Correct)

Rule 3: With a singular compound noun (for example, mother-in-law), show possession with an apostrophe + s at the end of the word.

Example

My mother-in-law's hat

If the compound noun (e.g., brother-in-law) is to be made plural, form the plural first (brothers-in-law), and then use the apostrophe + s.

Example

My two brothers-in-law's hats

Conjunctions and Punctuations

Rule 4a: If two people possess the same item, put the apostrophe + s after the second name only.

Example

Cesar and Seema's home is constructed of redwood.

However, if one of the joint owners is written as a pronoun, use the possessive form for both.

Example

Maribel and my home (Incorrect)
Mine and Seema's home (Incorrect)
Seema's and my home (Correct)
He and Seema's home (Incorrect)
Him and Seema's home (Incorrect)
His and Seema's home (Correct)
You and Seema's home (Incorrect)
Yours and Seema's home (Incorrect)
Seema's and your home (Correct)

Note: As the above examples demonstrate, when one of the co-owners is written as a pronoun, use possessive adjectives (my, your, her, our, their). Avoid possessive pronouns (mine, yours, hers, ours, theirs) in such constructions.

It should be mentioned that compound possessives are often clunky as well as confusing. For instance, a picture of her and Cesar's house could refer to a photo of "her" in front of the house that Cesar owns or a photo of the house that she and Cesar co-own. Big difference. Such ambiguous sentences should just be rewritten.

Rule 4b: In cases of separate rather than joint possession, use the possessive form for both.

Example

Cesar's and Maribel's homes are both lovely.
They don't own the homes jointly.
Cesar and Maribel's homes are both lovely.
The homes belong to both of them.

Rule 5: Use an apostrophe with contractions. The apostrophe is placed where a letter or letters have been removed.

Example

doesn't, it's, 'tis, can't, you'd, should've, rock 'n' roll, etc.
does'nt (Incorrect)

Rule 6: There are various approaches to plurals for abbreviations, single letters, and numerals.

Many writers and editors prefer an apostrophe after single capitalized letters.

Example

I made straight A's.

With groups of two or more capital letters, apostrophes seem less necessary.

Examples

There are two new MPs on the base.
He learned his ABCs.
She consulted with three M.D.s. Or She consulted with three M.D.'s.

Some write M.D.'s to give the s separation from the second period.

Single-digit numbers are usually spelled out, but when they aren't, you are just as likely to see 2s and 3s as 2's and 3's. With double digits and above, many (but not everyone) regard the apostrophe as superfluous: I scored in the high 90s.

There are different schools of thought about years and decades. The following examples are all in widespread use:

Example

the 1990s
the 1990's
the '90s
the 90's
the '90's (Awkward)

Rule 7: Amounts of time or money are sometimes used as possessive adjectives that require apostrophes.

Example

Three days leave (Incorrect)
Three days' leave (Correct)
My two cents worth (Incorrect)
My two cents' worth (Correct)

Rule 8: The personal pronouns hers, ours, yours, theirs, its, whose, and the pronoun oneself never take an apostrophe.

Example

Feed a horse grain. It's better for its health. (Correct)
Who's glasses are these? (Incorrect)
Whose glasses are these? (Correct)
Talking to one's self in public is odd. (Incorrect)
Talking to oneself in public is odd. (Correct)

Rule 9: When an apostrophe comes before a word or number, take care that it's truly an apostrophe (') rather than a single quotation mark (').

Example

'Twas the night before Christmas. (Incorrect)

'Twas the night before Christmas. (Correct)

I voted in '08. (Incorrect)

I voted in '08. (Correct)

> **Note:** Serious writers avoid the word 'til as an alternative to until. The correct word is till, which is many centuries older than until.

Rule 10: Beware of false possessives, which often occur with nouns ending in s. Don't add apostrophes to noun-derived adjectives ending in s. Close analysis is the best guide.

Example

We enjoyed the New Orleans' cuisine. (Incorrect)

In the preceding sentence, the word the makes no sense unless New Orleans is being used as an adjective to describe cuisine. In English, nouns frequently become adjectives. Adjectives rarely if ever take apostrophes.

Example

I like that Beatles' song. (Incorrect)

I like that Beatles song. (Correct) (Again, Beatles is an adjective, modifying song.)

He's a United States' citizen. (Incorrect)

He's a United States citizen. (Correct)

Rule 11: Beware of nouns ending in y; do not show possession by changing the y to ies.

Example

The company's policy (Correct)

The companies policy (Incorrect)

To show possession when a noun ending in y becomes plural, write ies'. Do not write y's.

Example

Three companies' policies (Correct)

Three company's policies (Incorrect)

Exception: Names and other proper nouns ending in 'y' become plural simply by adding an s. They do not form their plurals with an apostrophe, or by changing the *y* to *ies*.

Example

The Flannerys are coming over. (Correct)

The Flannery's are coming over. (Incorrect)

The Flanneries are coming over. (Incorrect)

The Flannerys' house was robbed. (Correct)

The Flanneries' house was robbed. (Incorrect)

MUST REMEMBER

- A conjunction joins words, phrases or sentences together.
- Coordinating conjunctions join two thoughts that are equally important in a sentence.
- Subordinating conjunctions are used to join two thoughts.
- Punctuation marks are symbols that are used to aid the clarity and comprehension of written language.
- Commas customarily indicate a brief pause; they're not as final as periods.
- Parentheses and brackets must never be used interchangeably.

PRACTICE EXERCISE

I. Fill in the blanks with the correct conjunction.

1. It was raining heavily, _____ we decided to cancel our dinner plans.
   (a) so   (b) for
   (c) or   (d) but

2. She wanted to participate in the school play _____ her father would not let her.
   (a) so   (b) for
   (c) or   (d) but

3. I did not go to the show _____ I had already seen it.
   (a) so   (b) as
   (c) or   (d) but

4. Read over your answers _____ correct all mistakes before you pass them up.
   (a) so   (b) for
   (c) and   (d) but

5. She had an unpleasant experience ____she was in London.
   (a) when   (b) although
   (c) that   (d) if

6. Joy welcomed his guests _____ offered them drinks.
   (a) so   (b) for
   (c) or   (d) and

7. She could not find the book she wanted _____ she borrowed a magazine instead.
   (a) so   (b) for
   (c) or   (d) but

8. Those village folks are poor _____ they seem contended always.
   (a) until   (b) though
   (c) unless   (d) because

9. _____ she hears she won, she will jump with joy.
   (a) if   (b) for
   (c) or   (d) but

10. I don't think he will remember to wish me _____ you remind him.
    (a) so   (b) if
    (c) until   (d) unless

II. Choose the correct option to join the following sentences.

1. We may have to take the airplane. Train tickets are not available.
   (a) since   (b) but
   (c) and   (d) so

2. You treated him badly. He is doing the same to you.
   (a) since   (b) but
   (c) and   (d) so

3. He is not feeling well. He refuses to take rest.
   (a) yet   (b) until
   (c) and   (d) so

4. He cannot afford to pay his fees. He is poor.
   (a) if   (b) as
   (c) and   (d) so

5. He contributed to the charity regularly. He was not rich.
   (a) since   (b) as
   (c) and   (d) although

6. Men may come or go. We are here forever.
   (a) since   (b) but
   (c) and   (d) so

7. Apologize to the whole class. You will be expelled.
   (a) since   (b) but
   (c) Otherwise (d) so

8. Nobody opened the door. He went away.
   (a) and   (b) so
   (c) for   (d) but

9. You promised to work hard. You continue to be lazy.
   (a) not   (b) or
   (c) yet   (d) so

10. Maya failed her test. She made many silly mistakes.
    (a) and   (b) or
    (c) yet   (d) because

III. Select the sentence which is correctly punctuated.

1. (a) Spain is a beautiful country; the beache's are warm, sandy and spotlessly clean.
   (b) Spain is a beautiful country: the beaches are warm, sandy and spotlessly clean.
   (c) Spain is a beautiful country, the beaches are warm, sandy and spotlessly clean.
   (d) Spain is a beautiful country; the beaches are warm, sandy and spotlessly clean.

2. (a) The children's books were all left in the following places: Mrs Smith's room, Mr Powell's office and the caretaker's cupboard.
   (b) The children's books were all left in the following places; Mrs Smith's room,

Mr Powell's office and the caretaker's cupboard.

(c) The childrens books were all left in the following places: Mrs Smiths room, Mr Powells office and the caretakers cupboard.

(d) The children's books were all left in the following places, Mrs Smith's room, Mr Powell's office and the caretaker's cupboard.

3. (a) She always enjoyed sweets, chocolate, marshmallows and toffee apples.
(b) She always enjoyed: sweets, chocolate, marshmallows and toffee apples.
(c) She always enjoyed sweets chocolate marshmallows and toffee apples.
(d) She always enjoyed sweet's, chocolate, marshmallow's and toffee apple's.

4. (a) I can't see Tim's car, there must have been an accident.
(b) I cant see Tim's car; there must have been an accident.
(c) I can't see Tim's car there must have been an accident.
(d) I can't see Tim's car; there must have been an accident.

5. (a) Tims gran, a formidable woman, always bought him chocolate, cakes, sweets and a nice fresh apple.
(b) Tim's gran a formidable woman always bought him chocolate, cakes, sweets and a nice fresh apple.
(c) Tim's gran, a formidable woman, always bought him chocolate cakes sweets and a nice fresh apple.
(d) Tim's gran, a formidable woman, always bought him chocolate, cakes, sweets and a nice fresh apple.

6. (a) After stealing Tims car, the thief lost his way and ended up the chief constable's garage.
(b) After stealing Tim's car the thief lost his way and ended up the chief constable's garage.
(c) After stealing Tim's car, the thief lost his way and ended up the chief constable's garage.
(d) After stealing Tim's car, the thief lost his' way and ended up the chief constable's garage.

7. (a) The potion contained: fruit, biscuits and glue.
(b) The potion contained fruit, biscuits and glue.
(c) The potion: contained fruit, biscuits and glue.
(d) None of these

8. (a) You have only one choice: leave now while you can.
(b) You have only one choice leave now while you can.
(c) You have only one choice. Leave now while you can.
(d) None of these

9. (a) I can see only one thing: the old lighthouse.
(b) I can see only one thing the old lighthouse.
(c) I can see: only one thing the old lighthouse.
(d) None of these

10. (a) In the bag were: scissors, a hairbrush and her address book.
(b) In the bag were the following: scissors, a hairbrush and her address book.
(c) In the bag there were: scissors, a hairbrush and her address book.
(d) None of these

11. (a) My favourite breakfast cereals are: corn flakes, frosties and golden nuggets.
(b) These are my favourite breakfast cereals: corn flakes, frosties and golden nuggets.
(c) My favourite breakfast cereals: corn flakes, frosties and golden nuggets.
(d) None of these

12. (a) I have only one thing to say to you: 'Get off my land.'
(b) The pot contained: sausages, mushrooms and beans.
(c) My favourite books are: 'On the Road' and 'The Naked Lunch'.
(d) My teacher used to say this: 'Always work hard but not too hard.'

13. (a) We have to stop: polluting the rivers, burning fossil fuels and using our cars.
(b) We have to stop doing these harmful things: polluting the rivers, burning fossil fuels and using our cars.
(c) These things cause environmental damage: polluting the rivers, burning fossil fuels and using our cars.
(d) Our quality of life is damaged by: polluting the rivers, burning fossil fuels and using our cars so much.

14. (a) The new house was: modern, spacious and luxurious.
    (b) Our new house looked: modern, spacious and luxurious.
    (c) I like a new house to be all of the following: modern, spacious and luxurious.
    (d) All the houses on the new estate were: modern, spacious and luxurious.

15. (a) Steve always went to watch football: he loved the atmosphere at the games.
    (b) Steve always went to watch football, he loved the atmosphere at the games.
    (c) Steve always went to watch football; he loved the atmosphere at the games.
    (d) None of these

16. (a) I love eating; eggs, bacon, cheese and toast.
    (b) I love eating eggs bacon cheese and toast.
    (c) I love eating eggs, bacon, cheese and toast.
    (d) None of these

17. (a) These are my favourite countries; Spain Hungary India and Greece.
    (b) These are my favourite countries: Spain, Hungary, India and Greece.
    (c) These are my favourite countries: Spain Hungary India and Greece.
    (d) None of these

18. (a) I love writing; English was always my favourite subject.
    (b) I love writing English; was always my favourite subject.
    (c) I love writing, English was always my favourite subject.
    (d) None of these

19. (a) Paul hates anything technical so, he never turns his computer on.
    (b) Paul hates anything technical, so he never turns his computer on.
    (c) Paul hates anything technical; so he never turns his computer on.
    (d) None of these

20. (a) John Paul's wife was kind, generous, clever and a fantastic cook.
    (b) John, Paul's wife, was kind generous clever and a fantastic cook.
    (c) John, Paul's wife, was a kind, generous, clever and fantastic cook.
    (d) None of these

21. (a) I love travelling: Spain, India, Thai-land and Hungary are my favourite countries.
    (b) I love travelling Spain, India, Thai-land and Hungary are my favourite countries.
    (c) I love travelling; Spain, India, Thai-land and Hungary are my favourite countries.
    (d) None of these

22. (a) "I love it to be here," he said. "It's so peaceful."
    (b) "I love it to be here," he said, It's so peaceful."
    (c) "I love it to be here" he said "It's so peaceful."
    (d) None of these

23. (a) 'Hands up!! This is a hold-up.'
    (b) He decided to hold-up the bank.
    (c) Could you hold-up the picture for me.
    (d) We were stuck in the huge hold-up on the M5.

24. (a) He lived in the eighteenth-century.
    (b) He had always been interested in the eighteenth-century.
    (c) He was fascinated by eighteenth-century history.
    (d) I love eighteenth-century architecture.

25. (a) His self-esteem was very low.
    (b) I hate self-assembly furniture.
    (c) He maintained his self-imposed silence.
    (d) It was clearly a case of self-defence.

26. (a) I prefer off-the-peg suits.
    (b) Could you take my coat off-the-peg?
    (c) I was made-to-measure the length of the classroom.
    (d) I prefer made-to-measure suits.

27. (a) The traffic was building-up badly.
    (b) He did not like being told-off.
    (c) I am going to finish-off that plate of chips.
    (d) Could you mop-up that mess in the corner please.

28. (a) Bristol's harbour is one of the countrys most beautiful place.
    (b) Bristols harbour is one of the country's most beautiful place.
    (c) Bristol's harbour is one of the country's most beautiful place.
    (d) Bristols' harbour is one of the countrys' most beautiful place.

29. (a) The two boy's bags were lying at the river's edge.
    (b) The two boys bag's were lying at the rivers' edge.

(c) The two boys' bags were lying at the river's edge.
(d) The two boys' bags' were lying at the rivers edge.

30. (a) My parent's flat is in one of the city's finest areas.
(b) My parents' flat is in one of the citys finest areas'.
(c) My parents' flat is in one of the citys' finest areas.
(d) My parents' flat is in one of the city's finest areas.

IV. **Choose the option which shows the correct contracted form of the given expression.**

1. (a) I am   — I'm
(b) I have   — I'm
(c) I will   — I've
(d) I would — I'll

2. (a) We have   — We're
(b) We will   — We'll
(c) We will not — We've
(d) We would   — Won't
(e) We are   — We'd

3. (a) She has   — She'll
(b) She will — She's
(c) She would — She's
(d) She is   — She's

4. (a) They are   — They've
(b) They would — They're
(c) They have — They've
(d) They will — They'w

5. (a) Who will — Who's
(b) Who would — Who's
(c) Who has   — Who'w
(d) Who is   — Who's

HOTS

I. **Choose the correct option which contains the pair(s) of clauses that can be connected with a semi-colon.**

1. (a) I hate rice pudding dairy products don't agree with me.
(b) Spain is lovely hot weather and friendly people.
(c) Spain lovely beaches, endless blue sea and great weather.
(d) Spain is a lovely country the beaches are endless and the weather is always good.

2. (a) Paris is a beautiful city wide streets and sunshine.
(b) Havana is a lovely city rice pudding is one of my favourite foods.
(c) I would love to go to France Paris is a lovely city.
(d) I would love to go to Greece I love ancient history.

3. (a) Understanding grammar is very important despite its complexity.
(b) Understanding grammar is very important clear communication is an essential skill.
(c) Understanding grammar is very important most high level jobs require good writing skills.
(d) Understanding grammar is very important although it is not always the most fascinating subject on the planet.

4. Which can/should be connected with a semi-colon?
(a) The stock exchange fell sharply investor confidence is very low.
(b) The stock exchange fell sharply many investors decided to sell their shares.
(c) The stock exchange fell sharply a difficult day for everybody.
(d) The stock exchange fell sharply I would wait before selling your shares.

5. (a) I'm not going on holiday this year I am very short of money.
(b) I'm not going on holiday this year no time!!
(c) I'm not going on holiday this year too expensive!
(d) I'm not going on holiday this year hot weather doesn't agree with me.

Tenses { 11 }

Learning Objectives : In this chapter, students will learn about:
- ✓ Usage of Tenses and its different types

CHAPTER SUMMARY

Tense is a reference of time. It indicates the time when a situation or event took place. There are three main types of tenses: present (now), past (before now) and future (after now).

Kinds of Tense

Simple Present Tense
Simple present tense is used for actions that happen on regular basis.

Examples
The boy **runs** very fast.
Mr. Roy **drives** his new car to office everyday.

Simple Past Tense
Simple past tense is used for an action that has already happened. It is usually accompanied by words such as yesterday, a week ago, last month, last year, etc.

Example
The dog **buried** a half-eaten bone in the garden yesterday.
I **completed** my project on time last week.

Simple Future Tense
Simple future tense is used to denote an action that will take place in future. It is usually used with the words 'shall' or 'will'.

Examples
I **will meet** you tomorrow.
I **shall study** for my exam tonight.

Present Continuous Tense
The present continuous tense is used for an action that is still going on.

Examples
I am **reading** Chetan Bhagat's novel.
The speech **is being delivered** now.

Past Continuous Tense
The past continuous tense is used for action that went on for some time in the past.

Examples
They **were waiting** for you all afternoon.
The boys **were playing** badminton while the girls were dancing.

Present Perfect Tense
The present perfect tense is used for an action that was completed just now, or an action started in the past and continuing in the present.

Examples
I **have** just **finished** my homework.
They **haven't lived** here for years.

> **TRIVIA**
> The dot over the letter 'i' is called Tittle. The dot is just called superscript dot. j is the another word.

Past Perfect Tense
The past perfect tense is used for an event that took place before another in the past. It is also called the 'had' tense.

Examples
John **had gone out** when I arrived in the office.

I **had saved** the document before the computer crashed.

Future Perfect Tense
The future perfect tense is used for an action that will be completed by a certain time in future.
Examples
I **shall have completed** my revision of all chapters by next week.
I **will have left** for home by the time he wakes up.

Past Perfect Continuous Tense
The past perfect continuous tense is used for an action that began in the past and continued up to a point.
Examples
Had you been waiting long before the taxi arrived?
It **had been raining hard** for several hours.

- Tense is a reference of time. It indicates the time when a situation or event took place.
- Simple past tense is used for an action that has already happened.
- Simple future tense is used to denote an action that will take place in future. It is usually used with the words 'shall' or 'will'.
- The present continuous tense is used for an action that is still going on.
- The past continuous tense is used for action that went on for some time in the past.

PRACTICE EXERCISE

Fill in the blanks with the correct form of present tense.

1. I have _____ with me all the necessary books.
   (a) brought   (b) bring
   (c) will bring   (d) bringing

2. We _____ a party last week.
   (a) hold   (b) held
   (c) will hold   (d) will be holding

3. We _____ our breakfast before we _____ for school.
   (a) eat/left   (b) ate/left
   (c) ate/leave   (d) eaten/left

4. The tree that had _____ on the roof _____ much damage.
   (a) fall/cause   (b) fell/caused
   (c) fallen/caused   (d) fall/caused

5. They _____ judo in the hall now.
   (a) are practicing (b) were practicing
   (c) practiced   (d) practice

6. I think he has seen us, and he _____ towards us.
   (a) come   (b) came
   (c) is coming   (d) will come

7. While the teacher _____, a lazy boy _____ at the back of the class.
   (a) taught/slept
   (b) teach/sleep
   (c) was teaching/was sleeping
   (d) will have taught/will have slept

8. It is a pity that Jenny _____ again.
   (a) fail   (b) failing
   (c) has failed   (d) had failed

9. Many people _____ this picture.
   (a) has never see   (b) never see
   (c) never saw   (d) have never seen

10. I hear that you just _____ your birthday?
    (a) celebrate   (b) will celebrate
    (c) celebrating   (d) celebrated

11. Did you _____ many friends?
    (a) invited   (b) inviting
    (c) invite   (d) invitation

12. This is the first time such a thing _____ here.
    (a) happens   (b) happened
    (c) happen   (d) happening

13. I think I _____ my pen.
    (a) lose   (b) have lost
    (c) has lost   (d) will lost

14. We _____ friends since childhood.
    (a) been   (b) has been
    (c) have been   (d) will be

15. This computer _____ with us for only a month.
    (a) have been   (b) has been
    (c) will been   (d) been

HOTS

Choose the correct tense of the following sentences.

1. He is sleeping. Do not disturb.
   (a) Present Continuous
   (b) Past Continuous
   (c) Present Perfect
   (d) Past Perfect

2. The sun rises in the east.
   (a) Simple Present (b) Simple Past
   (c) Simple Future   (d) Present Perfect

3. She enjoys reading books.
   (a) Simple Present (b) Simple Past
   (c) Simple Future   (d) Present Perfect

4. By the time you reach there, the train would have left.
   (a) Past Perfect   (b) Simple Past
   (c) Future Perfect (d) Present Perfect

5. By the end of this month, we will have completed the syllabus.
   (a) Past Perfect   (b) Simple Past
   (c) Future Perfect (d) Present Perfect

6. He lived in London last year.
   (a) Simple Present (b) Simple Past
   (c) Simple Future (d) Present Perfect
7. It will rain tomorrow.
   (a) Simple Present (b) Simple Past
   (c) Simple Future (d) Present Perfect
8. Are you still working for the same company?
   (a) Present Continuous
   (b) Past Continuous
   (c) Present Perfect
   (d) Past Perfect
9. They were waiting for the bus when the accident happened.
   (a) Present Continuous
   (b) Past Continuous
   (c) Present Perfect
   (d) Past Perfect
10. We have had the same car for ten years.
    (a) Past Perfect (b) Simple Past
    (c) Future Perfect (d) Present Perfect
11. She has worked in the bank for five years.
    (a) Past Perfect (b) Simple Past
    (c) Future Perfect (d) Present Perfect
12. The train had left when I arrived at the station.
    (a) Past Perfect (b) Simple Past
    (c) Future Perfect (d) Present Perfect
13. She had left the room when the police arrived.
    (a) Past Perfect (b) Simple Past
    (c) Future Perfect (d) Present Perfect
14. Are they visiting you next winter?
    (a) Present Continuous
    (b) Past Continuous
    (c) Present Perfect
    (d) Past Perfect
15. You will do exactly as I say.
    (a) Simple Present (b) Simple Past
    (c) Simple Future (d) Present Perfect
16. The water in the river will rise by a foot by evening, if the rain continues like this.
    (a) Past Perfect
    (b) Simple Past
    (c) Future Perfect
    (d) Present Perfect
17. We were not informed about what happened.
    (a) Past Perfect
    (b) Simple Past
    (c) Future Perfect
    (d) Present Perfect
18. They have been married for nearly fifty years.
    (a) Past Perfect
    (b) Simple Past
    (c) Future Perfect
    (d) Present Perfect
19. They were discussing where to go on a holiday when I visited them.
    (a) Present Continuous
    (b) Past Continuous
    (c) Present Perfect
    (d) Past Perfect
20. The Moon shines brightly at night.
    (a) Simple Present
    (b) Simple Past
    (c) Simple Future
    (d) Present Perfect

Voices and Narration — 12

Learning Objectives : In this chapter, students will learn about:
- ✓ Active Voice
- ✓ Passive Voice
- ✓ Direct and Indirect Speech

CHAPTER SUMMARY

"A Grammar of Contemporary English" defines Voice as "voice is a grammatical category which makes it possible to view the action of a sentence in two ways, without change in the facts reported". One and the same idea can often be expressed in two different ways, by means of an active, and a passive construction.

Active Voice

Active voice is used to indicate that the grammatical subject of the verb is performing the action or causing the happening denoted by the verb. With the active voice, you learn 'who' or 'what' is responsible for the action at the beginning of the sentence. In other words, the subject performs the action denoted by the verb. With help of active voice more powerful sentences can be build than passive voice.

Examples

Mansi reads a lesson.

Rohan plays football.

Uses of Active Voice

1. Active voice is used in a clause whose subject expresses the agent of the main verb.
2. Subject can be easily identified by asking 'who' or 'what' to the verb.
3. Sentences are short and easily understandable.

Example

John writes the letter.

John (subject) performs the action denoted by the verb (write).

Passive Voice

In passive voice the sentence focus on the object, i.e. who/what is receiving the action and not on who/what is performing the action. In passive voice, the actor of the of the verb (action) is either understood at the end of the sentence or maybe not told. The passive voice is used in writing facts, truth, lab or technical reports in which the does is not important or unknown, but the action happening on the object is very important.

Examples

A lesson is read by Mansi

Football is played by Rohan.

> **TRIVIA**
>
> The word "queue" is the only word in the English language that is still pronounced the same way when the last four letters are removed.

Uses of Passive Voice

1. Passive voice is used if we don't know the doer who is performing the job.
2. In the end of the clause or sentence "by" is prefixed to know the doer who is performing the job.
3. It is used if we are more interested in the job than the doers who work.

Example

The letter was written by John.

Letter receives the action denoted by the write (verb).

Identifying the Active/Passive Voice

Ask who/what performed the action (verb)? If the 'who or what is at the beginning of the sentence, the sentence is active voice.

Example

Jack is eating the apple.

Question will be : Who is eating the apple?

Look for the word 'by', if present it is passive voice.

Passive Voice Using Modals

The modal verbs consist of will, would, can, could, shall, should, may, might, must which are used with main verbs to express ability, probability, obligation, advice, etc.

To convert active voice having modal into passive voice, auxiliary verb "be" is added after modal in sentence.

Example

He can do this job. (Active Voice)

This job can be done by him. (Passive Voice)

Rules for Conversion of Active and Passive

Tense	Active Voice	Passive Voice
Simple Present Tense	Subject + V_1 OR V_1 + S/ES + object *Example:* The grocer sells fresh vegetables.	S + be + past participle + by object *Example:* Fresh vegetables are sold by the grocer.
Present Continuous Tense	Subject + be (is, am, are) + present participle + object *Example:* My boss is giving many assignments.	S + be (is, am, are) + being + past participle + by object *Example:* Many assignments are being given by my boss.
Present Perfect Tense	Subject + has/have + past participle + object *Example:* I have taken him out.	S + have/has been + past participle + by object *Example:* He has been taken out by me.
Simple Past Tense	Subject + past participle + object *Example:* He built a large house.	S + was/were + past participle + by object *Example:* A large house was built by him.
Past Continuous Tense	S + was/were + being + past participle + object *Example:* She was cooking dinner.	S + was/were + being + past participle + by object *Example:* Dinner was being cooked by her.
Past Perfect Tense	Subject + had + past participle + object *Example:* She had posted the letter.	S + had been + past participle + by object *Example:* The letter had been posted by her.
Simple Future Tense	Subject + will + V_1 + object *Example:* I will give you a present.	S + will + be + past participle + by object *Example:* A present will be given to you by me.
Future Perfect Tense	Subject + shall/will have + past participle + object *Example:* The doctor shall have examined ten patients by 10 o'clock.	S + shall/will have been + past participle + by object *Example:* Ten patients will have been examined by 10 o'clock by the doctor.

Voices and Narration

Rules for Changing Pronouns in Active to Passive conversion

Active Voice	Passive Voice
I	me
you	you
we	us
they	them
it	it

Pronoun: Number and Person

Number	Person I	Person II	Person III
Singular	I ⟶ am	you ⟶ are	he, she, it ⟶ is John, Sara ⟶ is
Plural	we ⟶ are	you ⟶ are	they ⟶ are

Uses of Passive

☞ Passive voice is used when the focus is on the action. It is not important or not known, however, who or what is performing the action.

Example

My bike was stolen.

In the above example, the focus is on the fact that my bike was stolen. I do not know, however, who did it.

☞ Sometimes a statement in passive is more polite than active voice, as the following example shows:

Example

A mistake was made.

In this case, I focus on the fact that a mistake was made, but I do not blame anyone (e.g. You have made a mistake.).

Formation of Passive Voice

Subject + finite form of verb + be + Past Participle (3rd column of irregular verbs)

Example

A letter was written.

When rewriting active voice in passive voice, note the following:

- The object of the active sentence becomes the subject of the passive sentence.
- The finite form of the verb is changed (be + past participle)
- The subject of the active sentence becomes the object of the passive sentence (or is dropped)

Examples

Tense	Voice	Subject	Verb	Object
Simple Present	Active	Rita	writes	a letter.
	Passive	A letter	is written	by Rita.
Simple Past	Active	Rita	wrote	a letter.
	Passive	A letter	was written	by Rita.

Present Perfect	Active	Rita	has written	a letter.
	Passive	A letter	has been written	by Rita.
Future	Active	Rita	will write	a letter.
	Passive	A letter	will be written	by Rita.
Modal	Active	Rita	can write	a letter.
	Passive	A letter	can be written	by Rita.

Other Examples

Tense	Voice	Subject	Verb	Object
Present Progressive	Active	Rita	is writing	a letter.
	Passive	A letter	is being written	by Rita.
Past Progressive	Active	Rita	was writing	a letter.
	Passive	A letter	was being written	by Rita.
Past Perfect	Active	Rita	had written	a letter.
	Passive	A letter	had been written	by Rita.
Future	Active	Rita	will have written	a letter.
	Passive	A letter	will have been written	by Rita.
Conditional I	Active	Rita	would write	a letter.
	Passive	A letter	would be written	by Rita.
Conditional II	Active	Rita	would have written	a letter.
	Passive	A letter	would have been written	by Rita.

Passive Voice with Two Objects

Rewriting an active voice with two objects in passive voice means that one of the two objects becomes the subject, the other one remains an object. Which object to transform into a subject depends on what you want to put the focus on.

Voice	Subject	Verb	Object 1	Object 2
Active	Rita	wrote	a letter	to me.
Passive	A letter	was written	to me	by Rita.
Passive	I	was written	a letter	by Rita.

Personal and Impersonal Passive

Personal Passive simply means that the object of the active sentence becomes the subject of the passive sentence. So, every verb that needs an object (transitive verb) can form a personal passive.

Example

They build houses. (Houses are built.)

Verbs without an object (intransitive verb) normally cannot form a personal passive sentence (as there is no object that can become the subject of the passive sentence). If you want to use an intransitive verb in passive voice, you need an impersonal construction – therefore this passive is called Impersonal Passive.

Example

He says. (It is said.)

Impersonal Passive is not as common in English as in some other languages (e.g. German, Latin).

In English, Impersonal Passive is only possible with verbs of perception (e. g. say, think, know).

Example

They say that women live longer than men. (It is said that women live longer than men.)

Although Impersonal Passive is possible here, Personal Passive is more common.

Example

They say that women live longer than men. (Women are said to live longer than men.)

The subject of the subordinate clause (women) goes to the beginning of the sentence; the verb of perception is put into passive voice. The rest of the sentence is added using an infinitive construction with 'to' (certain auxiliary verbs and that are dropped.

Direct and Indirect Speech

In our speech, we often speak to the other person of something that was said to us by somebody. In other words, we often report a speech whether ours or someone else's. We do this in two ways. We either report the speech exactly as we had heard or said it without making any change. This is called Direct Speech.

Example

The girl said to her mother, "My plate is empty."

We may change the sentence that we had heard or said without changing its meaning and then report it. This is called Indirect Speech.

Example

The girl said to her mother that her plate was empty.

> **Note:**
> While transforming from direct into indirect, we make several changes in a sentence:
> 1. We remove the comma in the indirect sentence and put that in its place.
> 2. We remove the inverted commas of the reported speech.
> 3. We change the 'my' of the reported speech into 'her'.
> 4. We do not any capital letter in between the sentence unlike in the direct form where the reported speech always begins with a capital letter.

Reporting Verb

The verb in first part of the sentence (he said, she said, he says, they said, she says,) before the statement of a person in sentence is called reporting verb.

Examples

He said, "I work in a factory". (Direct speech)

He said that he worked in a factory. (Indirect speech)

They said, "We are going to cinema." (Direct speech)

They said that they were going to cinema. (Indirect speech)

Reported Speech

The second part of indirect speech in which something has been told by a person (which is enclosed in quotation marks in direct speech) is called reported speech. For example, a sentence of indirect speech is: He said that he worked in a factory. In this sentence, the second part "he worked in a factory" is called reported speech and that is why the indirect speech as a whole can also be called reported speech.

Rules for Indirect Speech

Reported speech is not enclosed in quotation marks. Use of word "that": The word "that" is used as a conjunction between the reporting verb and reported speech.

Now, in order to bring about these changes while converting from direct into indirect or vice-versa, there are several important but simple rules that need to be observed. They are:

Change in Pronoun

The pronoun (subject) of the reported speech is changed according to the pronoun of reporting verb or object (person) of reporting verb (first part of sentence). Sometimes the pronoun may not change.

Rule 1: First person pronoun in reported speech i.e. I, we, me, us, mine, or our, is changed according to the pronoun of reporting verb if pronoun in reporting verb is third person pronoun i.e. he, she, it, they, him, his, her, them or their.

Examples

He said, "I live in New York." (Direct speech)

He said that he lived in New York. (Indirect speech)

They said, "We love our country." (Direct speech)

They said that they loved their country. (Indirect speech)

Rule 2: First person pronoun in reported speech i.e. I, we, me, us, mine, or our, is not changed if the pronoun (Subject) of reporting is also first person pronoun i.e. I or we.

Examples

I said, "I write a letter." (Direct speech)

I said that I wrote a letter. (Indirect speech)

We said, "We completed our work." (Direct speech)

We said that we completed our work. (Indirect speech)

Rule 3: Second person pronoun in reported speech i.e. you, yours is changed according to the person of object of reporting verb.

Example

She said to him, "You are intelligent." (Direct speech)

She said to him that he was intelligent. (Indirect speech)

He said to me, "You are late for the party." (Direct speech)

He said to me that I was late for the party. (Indirect speech)

Rule 4: Third person pronoun in reported speech i.e. he, she, it, they, him, his, her, them or their, is not changed in indirect speech.

Examples

They said, "He will come." (Direct speech)

They said that he would come. (Indirect speech)

You said, "They are waiting for the bus." (Direct speech)

You said that they were waiting for the bus. (Indirect speech)

Change in Time

Time is changed according to certain rules like now to then, today to that day, tomorrow to next day and yesterday to previous day.

Today	changes to	that day/the same day
Tomorrow	changes to	the next day/the following day
Yesterday	changes to	the day before/the previous day
Next week/month/year	changes to	the following week/month/year
Last week/month/year	changes to	the previous week/month/year
Now/just	changes to	then
Ago	changes to	before
Here	changes to	there
This	changes to	that

Examples

He said, "I am happy today." (Direct speech)

He said that he was happy that day. (Indirect speech)

Change in the Tense of Reported Speech

If the first part of sentence (reporting verb part) belongs to past tense the tense of reported speech will change. If the first part of sentence (reporting verb part) belongs to present or future tense, the tense of reported speech will not change.

Examples

He said, "I am happy." (Direct speech)

He said that he was happy. (Indirect speech) (Tense of reported speech changed)

He says, "I am happy." (Direct speech)

He said that he is happy. (Indirect speech) (Tense of reported speech didn't change)

Change in Tense of Reported Speech

Tense (Direct Speech)	Tense (Indirect Speech)
Present Simple Tense	Past Simple Tense
Present Continuous Tense	Past Continuous Tense
Present Perfect Tense	Past Perfect Tense
Present Perfect Continuous Tense	Past Perfect Continuous Tense
Past Simple Tense	Past Perfect Tense
Past Continuous Tense	Past Perfect Continuous Tense
Past Perfect Tense	Past Perfect Tense
Future Simple Tense, **will**	**would**
Future Continuous Tense, **will be**	**would be**
Future Perfect Tense, **will have**	**would have**

Examples

Direct Speech	Indirect Speech
He said, "I write a letter."	He said that he wrote a letter.
They said, "We love our country."	They said that they loved their country.
He said, "He is listening to the music."	He said that he was listening to the music.
They said, "We are enjoying the weather."	They said that they were not enjoying the weather.
She said, "He has finished his work."	She said that he had finished his work.
They said, "We have not gone to New York."	They said that they had not gone to New York.
He said, "I have been studying since 3 o'clock."	He said that he had been studying since 3 o'clock.
I said, "She has been working in this office since 2007."	I said that she had been working in this office since 2007.
John said, "They went to cinema."	John said that they had gone to cinema.
She said, "I didn't buy a car."	She said that she had not bought a car.
They said, "We were enjoying the weather."	They said that they had been enjoying.
I said, "It was raining."	I said that it had been raining.
She said, "She had visited a doctor."	She said that she had visited a doctor.
I said, "She had eaten the meal."	I said that she had eaten the meal.
He said, "I will study the book."	He said that he would study the book.
They said to me, "We will send you gifts."	They said to me that they would send you gifts.
I said to him, "I will be waiting for him."	I said to him that I would be waiting for him.
She said, "I will be shifting to new home."	She said that she would be shifting to a new home.
He said, "I will have finished the work."	He said that he would have finished the work.
She said, "They will have passed the examination."	She said that they would have passed the examination.

Note: The tense of reported speech may not change if reported speech is a universal truth though its reporting verb belongs to past tense.

Examples

He said, "Mathematics is a science." (Direct speech)

He said that mathematics is a science. (Indirect speech)

He said, "Sun rises in east." (Direct speech)

He said that sun rises in east. (Indirect speech) (Tense didn't change because reported speech is a universal truth though its reporting verb belongs to past tense)

Indirect Speech for Interrogative Sentences

For changing interrogative (question) sentence into indirect speech we have to observe the nature of question and then change it into indirect speech according to its rules for indirect speech. A question can be of two types. One which can be answered in only Yes or No and the other which needs a little bit explanation for its answer and cannot be answered in only Yes or No.

Examples

Do you like music? (It can be answered in Yes or No)

How are you? (It cannot be answered in Yes or No but it needs a little bit explanation, i.e., I am fine.)

Questions which can be answered in Yes/No in Indirect Speech

To change questions (which can be answered in yes or no) into indirect speech, word "if" or "whether" is used before the question in indirect speech. Rules for change in tense of question sentences are same as for change in normal tenses in indirect speech but sentence will not start with the auxiliary verb of the tense. The word "that" is not used between reporting verb and reported speech as conjunction in indirect speech for question sentence. Question mark is not used in indirect speech.

Examples

He said to me, "Do you like music?" (Direct speech)

He asked me if I liked music. (Indirect speech) (Not, did I like music)

or He asked me whether I liked music. (Indirect speech)

She said, "Will he participate in the quiz competition?" (Direct speech)

She asked me if he would participate in quiz competition. (Indirect speech)

I said to him, "Are you feeling well?" (Direct speech)

I asked him if he was feeling well. (Indirect speech)

They said to me, "Did you go to school?" (Direct speech)

They asked me if I had gone to school. (Indirect speech)

He said to me, "Have you taken the breakfast?" (Direct speech)

He asked me if I had taken the breakfast. (Indirect speech)

Questions which cannot be answered in Yees/No in Indirect Speech

To change such questions into indirect speech, the words "if" or "whether" is not used. The tense of the question is changed according to the rules for change in normal tenses in indirect speech but sentence will not start with the auxiliary verb of the tense. The word "that" is not used between reporting verb and reported speech as conjunction, in indirect speech for question sentence. Question mark is not used in indirect speech.

Examples

He said to me, "How are you?" (Direct speech)

He asked me how I was. (Indirect speech) (Not, how was I)

Teacher said to him, "What is your name?" (Direct speech)

Teacher asked him what his name was. (Indirect speech)

She said to him, "Why did you come late?" (Direct speech)

She asked him why he had come late. (Indirect speech)

He said, "When will they come?" (Direct speech)

Voices and Narration

He asked when they would come. (Indirect speech)

She asked her son, "Why are you crying?" (Direct speech)

She asked her son why he was crying. (Indirect speech)

Indirect Speech of Modals : Can, May, Must, Should, Ought to
These modals are changed to past forms.
- **Can** changes into **Could**
- **May** changes into **Might**
- **Must** changes into **Had to**

Examples

Direct Speech	Indirect Speech
He said, "I can drive a car."	He said that he could drive a car.
They said, "We can climb on a hill."	They said that they can climb on a hill.
He said, "I may buy a computer."	He said that he might buy a computer.
They said, "They may go to zoo."	They said that they might go to zoo.
He said, "I must work hard".	He said that he had to work hard.
She said, "They must carry on their work."	She said that they had to carry on their work.

Indirect speech of Modals : Should, Ought to, Might, Would and Could
These modals will not change in indirect speech
Examples

Direct Speech	Indirect Speech
Would	
They said, "We would apply for a visa."	They said that they would apply for visa.
He said, "I would start a business."	He said that he would start a business.
Could	
She said, "She could play a piano."	She said that she could play a violin.
They said, "We couldn't learn the lesson."	They said they couldn't learn the lesson.
Might	
He said, "Guests might come."	He said that guest might come.
John said, "I might meet him."	John said that he might meet him.
Should	
He said, "I should avail the opportunity."	He said that he should avail the opportunity.
They said, "We should take the exam."	They said that they should take the exam.
Ought to	
He said to me, "You ought to wait for him."	He said to me that I ought to wait for him.
They said, "We ought to attend our classes."	They said that they ought to attend their classes.

Indirect Speech of Imperative Sentence

A sentence which expresses command, request, advice or suggestion is called imperative sentence.

Examples

Open the door.

Please help me.

Learn your lesson.

To change such sentences into indirect speech, the word "ordered" or "requested" or "advised" or "suggested" or "forbade" or "not to do" is added to reporting verb depending upon nature of imperative sentence in reported speech.

Examples

He said to me, "Please help me." (Direct speech)

He requested me to help him. (Indirect speech)

She said to him, "You should work hard for exam." (Direct speech)

He suggested him to work hard for exam. (Indirect speech)

They said to him, "Do not tell a lie." (Direct speech)

They said to him not to tell a lie. (Indirect speech)

He said, "Open the door." (Direct speech)

He ordered to open the door. (Indirect speech)

Indirect Speech of Exclamatory Sentences

Sentence which expresses state of joy or sorrow or wonder is called exclamatory sentence.

Examples

Hurrah! We won the match.

Alas! I failed the test.

Wow! What a nice shirt it is.

To change such sentences, the words "exclaimed with joy" or "exclaimed with sorrow" or "exclaimed with wonder" is added in the reporting verb depending upon the nature of exclamatory sentence in indirect speech.

Examples

He said, "Hurrah! I won a prize." (Direct speech)

He exclaimed with joy that he had won a prize. (Indirect speech)

She said, "Alas! I failed in exam." (Direct speech)

She exclaimed with sorrow that she failed in the exam. (Indirect speech)

John said, "Wow! What a nice shirt it is." (Direct speech)

John exclaimed with wonder that it was a nice shirt. (Indirect speech)

She said, "Hurrah! I am selected for the job." (Direct speech)

She exclaimed with joy that she was selected for the job. (Indirect speech)

MUST REMEMBER

- Active voice is used to indicate that the grammatical subject of the verb is performing the action or causing the happening denoted by the verb.
- In passive voice the sentence focus on the object, i.e. who/what is receiving the action and not on who/what is performing the action.
- Passive voice is used when the focus is on the action.
- The verb in first part of the sentence (he said, she said, he says, they said, she says,) before the statement of a person in sentence is called reporting verb.
- The second part of indirect speech in which something has been told by a person (which is enclosed in quotation marks in direct speech) is called reported speech.

Voices and Narration

PRACTICE EXERCISE

I. Choose the option which contains the correct passive/active voice of the given sentence.

1. He can speak French.
   (a) French can spoken by him.
   (b) French can be spoke by him.
   (c) French can be spoken by him.
   (d) French could be spoken by him.

2. They may win the battle.
   (a) The battle may be win.
   (b) The battle may be won.
   (c) The battle may be won by them.
   (d) The battle may won.

3. Nobody can catch him.
   (a) He can not be caught.
   (b) He can not caught.
   (c) He could not be cought.
   (d) He could not cought.

4. We must have obeyed our teachers.
   (a) Our teachers might have obeyed.
   (b) Our teachers might have been obeyed.
   (c) Our teachers must have been obeyed.
   (d) Our teachers must have obeyed.

5. Rahul must have done that task.
   (a) That task must had been done by Rahul.
   (b) That task must have been done by Rahul.
   (c) That task must have done by Rahul.
   (d) That task must have been did by Rahul.

6. We ought to have saved our environment.
   (a) Our environment ought to had been saved.
   (b) Our environment ought to have been save.
   (c) Our environment ought to have been saved.
   (d) Our environment ought to have saved.

7. There is no book to read.
   (a) To be read there is no book.
   (b) To read there is no book.
   (c) There is no book to read.
   (d) There is no book to be read.

8. There is nothing to do.
   (a) There was nothing to be done.
   (b) There is nothing to be done.
   (c) There is nothing to done.
   (d) There is no thing to do.

9. It is time to prepare for the game trails.
   (a) It is time to prepared for the game trails.
   (b) It is time to be prepared for the game trails.
   (c) It is time for the game trails to prepared.
   (d) It is time for the game trails to be prepared.

10. It is time to learn English.
    (a) It is time to be learnt English.
    (b) It is time for English to be learnt.
    (c) It is time for English to learnt.
    (d) It is time to be learn English.

11. It is time to do our business.
    (a) It is time for our business to be done.
    (b) It is time to our business to be done.
    (c) It is time our business to be done.
    (d) It is time for our business be done.

12. He likes people to respect him.
    (a) He like respect.
    (b) He likes to be respected.
    (c) He like to be respected.
    (d) He want to be respected.

13. Rohit has to see it or to believe it.
    (a) It has to be saw or to be believe by Rohit.
    (b) It has to be seen or to believe by Rohit.
    (c) It has to be seen or to be believed by Rohit.
    (d) It has to be seen or to be believe by Rohit.

14. Switch on the cooler.
    (a) Let cooler be switch on.
    (b) Switch on the cooler please.
    (c) Let cooler be switched on.
    (d) Let the cooler be switched on.

15. Bring the bottle of juice.
    (a) Let a bottle of juice be brought.
    (b) Let the bottle of juice be brought.
    (c) Let a bottle of juice brought.
    (d) Let a bottle of juice be bring.

16. Don't insult the deaf man.
    (a) Let the deaf man not be insult.
    (b) Let the deaf man not be insulted.
    (c) Let the deaf man not insulted.
    (d) Let deaf man not be insulted.
17. Don't touch the fence.
    (a) Let the fence not be touch.
    (b) Let the fence not be touched.
    (c) Let the fence not touched.
    (d) Let the fence to not be touched.
18. Help the poor.
    (a) The poor should helped.
    (b) We should help poor.
    (c) Let the poor be helped.
    (d) The poor should be helped.
19. Respect your neighbours.
    (a) Your neighbours should respected.
    (b) Your neighbours should be respected.
    (c) Let neighbours be respected.
    (d) Let neighbours respected.
20. Please give me a pen.
    (a) You are ordered to give me a pen.
    (b) You are ought to give me a pen.
    (c) You are requested to give me pen.
    (d) You are requested to give me a pen.
21. Please tell me something.
    (a) You are requested to tell me something.
    (b) You are requested tell me something.
    (c) You are requested to tell something.
    (d) You are request to tell me something.
22. This shirt cannot be worn by me any longer.
    (a) I cannot wear this shirt any longer.
    (b) Wearing of this shirt any longer is not possible.
    (c) This shirt is too worn out any longer.
    (d) This worn out shirt cannot be worn any longer.
23. Lion does not eat grass, however hungry he may be.
    (a) Grass is not eaten by a lion, however hungry he may be.
    (b) Grass was being not eaten by a lion, however hungry he may be.
    (c) Grass is eaten not by a lion, however hungry he may be.
    (d) Grass is not being eaten by a lion, however hungry he may be.
24. Someone saw him picking up a gun.
    (a) He was seen pick up a gun by someone.
    (b) He was seen picking up a gun by someone.
    (c) He is seen picking up a gun by someone.
    (d) He was seen by someone pick a gun.
25. He was obliged to resign.
    (a) He was make to resign.
    (b) To resign was his obligation.
    (c) Circumstances obliged him to resign.
    (d) Registration obliged him.
26. Why did you not agree to my proposal?
    (a) Why was my proposal not agreed to?
    (b) Why was my proposal not agreed by you?
    (c) Why my proposal was not agreed to by you?
    (d) Why was my proposal not agreed to by you?
27. Do you understand what I mean?
    (a) What I mean is that understood by you?
    (b) Was what I mean understood by you?
    (c) Is what I mean is understood by you?
    (d) What I mean is understood by you?
28. Whom does he look for?
    (a) Whom he is looked after for?
    (b) Who is looked after for him?
    (c) Who is looked for by him?
    (d) Whom he looked after by?
29. They say that you did that.
    (a) You are told to do that.
    (b) You are advised to do that.
    (c) You did that said by them.
    (d) You are said to have done that.
30. I am doing sums.
    (a) Sums are done by me.
    (b) Sums are being done by me.
    (c) I must be doing the sum.
    (d) Sums must be done by me.
31. The noise of traffic kept me awake.
    (a) I was kept awake by the noise of the traffic.

Voices and Narration

(b) The traffic kept me awake by noise.
(c) I kept myself awake due to the noise of the traffic.
(d) I remained awake by the noise of the traffic.

32. He was congratulated by his teacher on his brilliant success in the recent examination.
    (a) He congratulated his teacher on his brilliant success in the examination.
    (b) His teacher congratulated him for his brilliant success in the recent examination.
    (c) His teacher congratulated him on his brilliant success in the examination.
    (d) His teacher congratulated him.

33. People speak English all over the world.
    (a) English is spoken all over the world.
    (b) English was spoken all over the world.
    (c) English was spoken by people.
    (d) English is spoken by people.

34. Who gave you permission to enter?
    (a) By whom were you given permission to enter?
    (b) By whom was you given permission to enter?
    (c) By whom you were given permission to enter?
    (d) By whom were given you permission to enter?

35. The principal has granted him a scholar-ship.
    (a) A scholarship has granted to him by the principal.
    (b) He has been granted a scholarship by the Principal.
    (c) He has granted a scholarship by the Principal.
    (d) A scholarship was granted to him by the principal.

36. Before festivals the shops are thronged with men, women and children making various purchase.
    (a) During festival people throng the shops.
    (b) Men, women and children throng the shops before festival making various purchases.
    (c) Men, women and children make purchases during festivals.
    (d) The shops are thronged by people making purchases.

37. The accountant took the money from the customer.
    (a) The money is taken from the customer by the accountant.
    (b) The money was taken from the customer by the accountant.
    (c) The customer was taken the money by the accountant.
    (d) The money had been taken from the customer by the accountant.

38. The peon refused him admittance.
    (a) He was refused admittance by the peon.
    (b) Admittance is refused to him by the peon.
    (c) Admittance was refused by the peon to him.
    (d) Admittance is refused him by the peon.

39. The boy has rung the bell.
    (a) The bell has been rung by the boy.
    (b) The bell was being rung by the boy.
    (c) The bell was rung by the boy.
    (d) The bell has been being rung by the boy.

40. They made him a king.
    (a) A king has been made by him.
    (b) He was made a king by them.
    (c) They have been made king by him.
    (d) He has been made a king by them.

II. Choose the option which best expresses the given sentence in Indirect/Direct speech.

1. The boy said, "Who dare call you a thief?"
   (a) The boy enquired who dared call him a thief.
   (b) The boy asked who called him a thief.
   (c) The boy told that who dared call him a thief.
   (d) The boy wondered who dared call a thief.

2. She exclaimed with sorrow that was a very miserable plight.
   (a) She said with sorrow, "What a pity it is."
   (b) She said, "What a mystery it is."
   (c) She said, "What a miserable sight it is."
   (d) She said, "What a miserable plight it is."

3. Dhruv said that he was sick and tired of working for that company.
   (a) Dhruv said, "I am sick and tired of working for this company."
   (b) Dhruv said, "He was tired of that company."
   (c) Dhruv said to me, "I am sick and tired of working for this company."
   (d) Dhruv said, "I will be tired of working for that company."

4. "Are you alone, my son?" asked a soft voice close behind me.
   (a) A soft voice asked that what I was doing there alone.
   (b) A soft voice said to me are you alone son.
   (c) A soft voice from my back asked If I was alone.
   (d) A soft voice behind me asked if I was alone.

5. She said to him, "Why don't you go today?"
   (a) She asked him why he did not go that day.
   (b) She said to him why he don't go that day.
   (c) She asked him not to go that day.
   (d) She asked him why he did not go today.

6. He exclaimed with joy that India had won the Sahara Cup.
   (a) He said, "India has won the Sahara Cup"
   (b) He said, "India won the Sahara Cup"
   (c) He said, "How! India will win the Sahara Cup"
   (d) He said, "Hurrah! India has won the Sahara Cup"

7. The little girl said to her mother, "Did the sun rise in the East?"
   (a) The little girl said to her mother that the sun rose in the East.
   (b) The little girl asked her mother if the sun rose in the East.
   (c) The little girl said to her mother if the sun rises in the East.
   (d) The little girl asked her mother if the sun is in the East.

8. The man said, "No, I refused to confess guilt."
   (a) The man emphatically refused to confess guilt.
   (b) The man refused to confess his guilt.
   (c) The man told that he did not confess guilt.
   (d) The man was stubborn enough to confess guilt.

9. Rani ordered her servant to bring her a cup of tea.
   (a) Rani told her servant, "Bring a cup of tea."
   (b) Rani said, "Bring me a cup of tea."
   (c) Rani said to her servant, "Bring me a cup of tea."
   (d) Rani told her servant, "Bring her that cup of tea."

10. My cousin said, "My room-mate had snored throughout the night."
    (a) My cousin said that her room-mate snored throughout the night.
    (b) My cousin told me that her room-mate snored throughout the night.
    (c) My cousin complained to me that her room-mate is snoring throughout the night.
    (d) My cousin felt that her room-mate may be snoring throughout the night.

11. "Please don't go away", she said.
    (a) She said to please her and not go away.
    (b) She told me to go away.
    (c) She begged me not to go away.
    (d) She begged that I not go away.

12. She said to her friend, "I know where is everyone"
    (a) She told that she knew where was everyone.
    (b) She told her friend that she knew where was everyone.
    (c) She told her friend that she knew where is everyone.
    (d) She told her friend that she knows where was everyone.

13. Sushant said to him, "I have been helping your son for years".
    (a) Sushant told him that he has helped his son for years.
    (b) Sushant told him that he have been helping his son for years.
    (c) Sushant told him that he had been helping his son for years.
    (d) Sushant told him that he has been helping his son for years.

14. He said to me, "I shall write an essay".
    (a) He said to me that he will be writing an essay.
    (b) He told me that he would write an essay.
    (c) He said to me that he will write an essay.
    (d) He told me that he would write an essay.

Voices and Narration

15. He said to me, "I shall be writing an essay".
    (a) He told me that he would have been writing an essay.
    (b) He told me that he would be writing an essay.
    (c) He told me that he will be writing an essay.
    (d) He told me that he shall be writing an essay.
16. Sita said to Geeta, "You can learn piano".
    (a) Sita told Geeta that she can be learn piano.
    (b) Sita told Geeta that you can learn piano.
    (c) Sita told Geeta that she could learn piano.
    (d) Sita told Geeta that she can learn piano.
17. He said to you, "You may go out".
    (a) He told you that you might be go out.
    (b) He said you that you might be go out.
    (c) He told you that you may go out.
    (d) He told you that you might go out.
18. Ram said to Rahul, "You are a good player of cricket".
    (a) Ram told Rahul that he was a good player of cricket.
    (b) Ram told Rahul that he were a good player of cricket.
    (c) Ram told Rahul that he would a good player of cricket.
    (d) Ram told Rahul that he could be a good player of cricket.
19. Ramakant said to me, "I have no time for you".
    (a) Ramakant said that he had no time for me.
    (b) Ramakant told me that he had no time for me.
    (c) Ramakant told me that he has no time for me.
    (d) Ramakant told me that he was having no time for me.
20. Sahil said to Vipul, "I was going to buy milk".
    (a) Sahil told Vipul that he were going to buy milk.
    (b) Sahil told Vipul that he would going to buy milk.
    (c) Sahil told Vipul that he had been going to buy milk.
    (d) Sahil told Vipul that he was going to buy milk.
21. She said, "You were missing from the picnic".
    (a) She told me that I had been missing from the picnic.
    (b) She told me that I has been missing from the picnic.
    (c) She told me that I were missing from the picnic.
    (d) She told me that I had been missed from the picnic.
22. Reeta said to Shivani, "You have to go to school".
    (a) Reeta told Shivani that she would have to go to school.
    (b) Reeta told Shivani that she has to go to school.
    (c) Reeta told Shivani that she have to go to school.
    (d) Reeta told Shivani that she had to go to school.
23. You said to her, "She has to cook food for you".
    (a) You told her that she has to cook food for you.
    (b) You told her that she had to cook food for you.
    (c) You told her that she needs to cook food for you.
    (d) You told her that she would have to cook food for you.
24. He said to me, " I had to finish this first."
    (a) He told me that he has to finish this first.
    (b) He told me that he have to finish this first.
    (c) He told me that he had had to finish this first.
    (d) He told me that he had to finish this first.
25. Rahul said to Sunita, "I had to reach there".
    (a) Rahul told Sunita that he has to reach there.
    (b) Rahul told Sunita that he would have to reach there.
    (c) Rahul told Sunita that he had to reach there.
    (d) Rahul told Sunita that he had had to reach there.
26. She said to me, "I could reach there easily".
    (a) She told me that she could reach there easily.
    (b) She told me that she could have reach there easily.

(c) She told me that she had reach there easily.
(d) She told me that she had been reach there easily.

27. Reena said to Jitender, "You would not fight with me."
    (a) Reena told to Jitender that he has not to fight with her.
    (b) Reena told to Jitender that he would not fight with her.
    (c) Reena told to Jitender that he will not fight with her.
    (d) Reena told to Jitender that he should not fight with her.

28. My father said to me, "It might rain yesterday".
    (a) My father told me that it may have rain the previous day.
    (b) My father told me that it would rain the previous day.
    (c) My father told me that it might rain the previous day.
    (d) My father told me that it could rain the previous day.

29. He said, "I went to Rajasthan yesterday."
    (a) He told that he had gone to Rajasthan the day before.
    (b) He told that he has gone to Rajasthan the day before.
    (c) He told that he has went to Rajasthan the day before.
    (d) He told that he had went to Rajasthan the day before.

30. Raju said to me, "He worked hard".
    (a) Raju told me that he had worked hard.
    (b) Raju told me that he has worked hard.
    (c) Raju told me that he had been worked hard.
    (d) Raju told me that he has been worked hard.

31. Rahul said, "He was walking."
    (a) Rahul said that he had been walking.
    (b) Rahul said that he was walking.
    (c) Rahul said that he had walking.
    (d) Rahul said that he had walked.

32. Sheela said to me, "Munni is dancing better than me."
    (a) Sheela told me that Munni have been dancing better than her.
    (b) Sheela told me that Munni was dancing better than her.
    (c) Sheela told me that Munni had been dancing better than her.
    (d) Sheela told me that Munni had dancing better than her.

33. She said, "He was trying to help me".
    (a) She said that he tried to help her.
    (b) She said that he had been trying to help her.
    (c) She said that he has been trying to help her.
    (d) She said that he was trying to help her.

34. Deepak said to me, "I had finished the coffee."
    (a) Deepak told me that he had finished the coffee.
    (b) Deepak told me that he had been finished the coffee.
    (c) Deepak told me that he had finish the coffee.
    (d) Deepak told me that he finished the coffee.

35. Rahul said to me, "I had gone through it."
    (a) Rahul told me that he have went through it.
    (b) Rahul told me that he have gone through it.
    (c) Rahul told me that he had went through it.
    (d) Rahul told me that he had gone through it.

36. Ravinder said to me, "I had been working on it for 5 days."
    (a) Ravinder told me that he had been working on it for 5 days.
    (b) Ravinder told me that he has been working on it for 5 days.
    (c) Ravinder told me that he had worked on it for 5 days.
    (d) Ravinder told me that he was working on it for 5 days.

37. Sweeta said to me, "I had been writing an essay for 3 hours."
    (a) Sweeta told me that she has been writing an essay for 3 hours.
    (b) Sweeta told me that she had been writing an essay for 3 hours.
    (c) Sweeta told me that she was writing an essay for 3 hours.
    (d) Sweeta told me that she had written an essay for 3 hours.

Voices and Narration

38. Rahul said, "I can buy that watch."
    (a) Rahul said that he can buy that watch.
    (b) Rahul said that he could buy that watch.
    (c) Rahul said that he was able to buy that watch.
    (d) Rahul said that he can be buy that watch.
39. He said, "Honesty is the best policy."
    (a) He said that Honesty is the best policy.
    (b) He said that Honesty was the best policy.
    (c) He said that Honesty would be the best policy.
    (d) He said that Honesty will be the best policy.
40. He remarked, "Two and two makes four."
    (a) He remarked that two and two would make four.
    (b) He remarked that two and two made four.
    (c) He remarked that two and two makes four.
    (d) He advised that two and two makes four.

HOTS

Direction: Choose the most suitable passive voice conversions of the given sentences:

1. The manager will give you a ticket.
   (a) A ticket will be given to you by the manager.
   (b) You will be given a ticket by the manager.
   (c) Both (a) and (b)
   (d) None of the above.
2. We saw you and him.
   (a) You and him was seen by us.
   (b) You and he were seen by us.
   (c) You and him were seen by us.
   (d) You and he seen by us.
3. Give the order for one hundred calendars.
   (a) Let the order for one hundred calendars be given.
   (b) Order for one hundred calendars should be given.
   (c) Both (a) and (b)
   (d) None of the above.
4. Call the ambulance at once.
   (a) Let the ambulance called at once.
   (b) The ambulance should be called at once.
   (c) Let the ambulance be called at once.
   (d) Both (b) and (c)
5. Mrs. Smith looks after her children very well.
   (a) Her children looked very well by Mrs. Smith.
   (b) Her children are looked very well by Mrs. Smith.
   (c) Her children are looked after very well by Mrs. Smith.
   (d) None of these

Vocabulary   13

Learning Objectives : In this chapter, students will learn about:
- ✓ Words related to travel, leisure, locations and Activities

CHAPTER SUMMARY

Words can be grouped into different categories. Let's learn about three categories and see how many words we can come up with for each of them.

TRIVIA

"Shit" is among the oldest of English Language which mean "cattle diarrhoea".

Words related to Travel and Leisure

Airport	Abroad	Accommodations	Airfare
Amenities	Board	Beach	Boathouse
Budget	Bon Voyage	Bus Station	Cafe
Camping	Cancellation	Check-In	Cruise
Coach	Destination	Excursion	Expedition
Fly	Ferry	Globetrotter	Hotel
Hiking	Horseback Riding	International	Journey
Landing	Luggage	Location	Lodging
Plane	Passenger	Route	Railway
Road	Reservation	Return Ticket	Resort
Refreshment	Sightseeing	Suitcase	Sail
Sea	Ship	Safari	Sanctuary
Take-Off	Travel Agent	Trip	Tour
Tourist	Traffic	Train	Taxi
Voyage	Vacation		

Vocabulary   113

Words related to Locations and Places

Apartment	Area	Bungalow	Building
Bakery	Block	Bay	Beach
Cottage	Castle	Church	Cathedral
Cliff	Coast	Countryside	City
Country	Capital	Centre	District
Fire Station	Forest	House	Hotel
Hospital	Hill	Lake	Mountain
Office	Outskirts	Park	Post Office
Police Station	Port	River	Restaurant
Railway Station	Residence	Resort	Rural
Region	Skyscraper	Shop	Shopping Mall
Suburb	Sea	Seaside	Shore
Stream	School	Town	Urban
Village	Valley	Woods	

Words related to Activities

Act	Accelerate	Analyze	Advise
Arrange	Adjust	Bend	Blink
Creep	Crawl	Catch	Climb
Clap	Compose	Construct	Discover
Design	Derive	Detect	Develop
Dig	Dive	Dance	Earn
Entertain	Exercise	Explore	Gallop
Grab	Hop	Invent	Illustrate
Jump	Jog	Kick	Locate
Leap	Listen	March	Operate
Participate	Perform	Produce	Pull
Push	Punch	Roll	Ride
Run	Skip	Sway	Swing
Shake	Stamp	Shuffle	Swim

Skate	Search	Solve	Study
Stomp	Train	Teach	Twist
Twirl	Tip-Toe	Throw	Turn
Wiggle	Walk	Wave	Write
Wink	Yawn	Yell	

- A vocabulary is a set of familiar words within a person's language.
- A vocabulary serves as a useful and fundamental tool for communication and acquiring knowledge.

PRACTICE EXERCISE

I. Fill in the blanks with the most appropriate word.

1. _____ are quite high these days. But they are often slashed during the festive seasons.
   (a) airfares   (b) international
   (c) hotel   (d) passport

2. My uncle is a _____. He travelled to fifteen countries in the past six months.
   (a) passenger   (b) tourist
   (c) globetrotter   (d) travel agent

3. I have signed up for an _____ to Mt Everest. However, I need to go through some physical training before that.
   (a) sightseeing   (b) expedition
   (c) voyage   (d) vacation

4. The main attraction of the Jim Corbett National Park is the wildlife _____.
   (a) tour   (b) ferry
   (c) cruise   (d) safari

5. We usually say _____ to a person setting off on a journey.
   (a) bon voyage   (b) check in
   (c) take off   (d) sail

6. I came to the mountains because I love _____ up the hills on foot.
   (a) biking   (b) hiking
   (c) skiing   (d) riding

7. My parents have visited all the states in India. Next year they are planning to go _____.
   (a) board   (b) road
   (c) route   (d) abroad

8. She caught the last _____ across the river just before sunset.
   (a) taxi   (b) train
   (c) ferry   (d) bus

9. In order to cut down expenditure, Jess decided to not stay in a _____, but go _____ instead.
   (a) hotel/camping
   (b) camp/hotel
   (c) hotel/resort
   (d) hotel/boathouse

10. There's a new bird _____ near my house. You can spot many rare species there.
    (a) safari   (b) sanctuary
    (c) destination   (d) lodging

II. Fill in the blanks with the correct option.

1. Standing at the edge of the _____, we watched the waves crash on the shore far below.
   (a) cliff   (b) beach
   (c) lake   (d) port

2. In the evenings, he loves to watch the children play in the _____ across the street.
   (a) road   (b) country
   (c) park   (d) forest

3. The authorities have decided to cut down the _____ to make way for a new roadway.
   (a) hill   (b) forest
   (c) river   (d) sea

4. I visited a _____ this morning where the priest was a woman.
   (a) city   (b) town
   (c) park   (d) church

5. New Delhi is to India, like London is to United Kingdom. They are the _____ cities.
   (a) capital   (b) country
   (c) city   (d) countryside

6. According to the weather forecast, the typhoon is likely to approach the _____.
   (a) residence   (b) district
   (c) coast   (d) bay

7. Although considered to be a holy _____, not enough is done to keep the Ganges clean.
   (a) river   (b) town
   (c) city   (d) coast

8. Tom baked over a 100 cupcakes this afternoon. He plans to open a _____ of his own very soon.
   (a) hospital   (b) bakery
   (c) school   (d) post office

9. I waited at the _____ for more than an hour to lodge a complaint against the robbery at my apartment.
   (a) school (b) restaurant
   (c) post office (d) police station
10. These days, people prefer to go to _____ more than meeting up with friends and relatives.
   (a) cottage (b) shopping mall
   (c) outskirts (d) port

III. Choose the correct option which describes the given expression.
1. A very tall building in a city
   (a) school (b) post office
   (c) skyscraper (d) block
2. A place where sick or injured people are given care or treatment
   (a) house (b) hospital
   (c) church (d) resort
3. An area of low land between hills or mountains
   (a) valley (b) beach
   (c) coast (d) stream
4. Relating to country, rather than city
   (a) urban (b) forest
   (c) outskirts (d) rural
5. A large building with high, thick walls and towers that was built in the past to protect against attack
   (a) church (b) cathedral
   (c) castle (d) cottage

HOTS

Choose the correct option (in column B) which describes the given picture (in column A)

S. No	Column A	Column B
1.		(a) roll (b) twist (c) crawl (d) tiptoe
2.		(a) swim (b) dive (c) dig (d) jump

3.		(a) kick (b) run (c) leap (d) hop
4.		(a) sway (b) wave (c) swirl (d) dance
5.		(a) roll (b) skate (c) ride (d) shuffle
6.		(a) ride (b) leap (c) gallop (d) hop
7.		(a) listen (b) invent (c) develop (d) discover

8.		(a) perform (b) construct (c) exercise (d) study
9.		(a) sleep (b) yawn (c) yell (d) wiggle
10.		(a) wink (b) blink (c) twirl (d) sway

Vocabulary

SECTION 2
READING COMPREHENSION

Reading Comprehension – I

NEWS STORIES

I. Read the news article and answer the questions that follow.

Japan Earthquake: Tsunami Hits North-east

TOKYO, 11 March 2011: Japan's most powerful earthquake since records began has struck the north-east coast, triggering a massive tsunami. Cars, ships and buildings were swept away by a wall of water after the 8.9-magnitude tremor, which struck about 400km (250 miles) north-east of Tokyo. A state of emergency has been declared at the Fukushima nuclear power plant, where pressure has exceeded normal levels.

Officials say 350 people are dead and about 500 missing, but it is feared the final death toll will be much higher. The quake was the fifth-largest in the world since 1900 and nearly 8,000 times stronger than the one which devastated Christchurch, New Zealand, last month, said scientists. Thousands of people living near the Fukushima nuclear power plant have been ordered to evacuate. In the centre of Tokyo many people are spending the night in their offices. But thousands, perhaps millions, chose to walk home. Train services were suspended. Even after the most violent earthquake anyone could remember the crowds were orderly and calm. The devastation is further to the north, along the Pacific coast. There a tsunami triggered by the quake reached 10km (six miles) inland in places carrying houses, buildings, boats and cars with it. In the city of Sendai the police found up to 300 bodies in a single ward. Outside the city in a built-up area a fire blazed across several kilometres. Japan's ground self-defence forces have been deployed, and the government has asked the US military based in the country for help. The scale of destruction from the biggest quake ever recorded in Japan will become clear only at first light.

1. What is the magnitude of the terror felt?
   (a) 9.8   (b) 8.9
   (c) 7.8   (d) 8.7

2. A state emergency has been declared at the _____ nuclear plant.
   (a) Fukushima
   (b) Fakashima
   (c) Kukushima
   (d) Fikusina

3. The passage talks about another quake that happened a month ago. Where did it take place?
   (a) Australia   (b) China
   (c) Japan   (d) New Zealand

4. How were the crowds behaving after facing the massive quake?
   (a) they were panicking
   (b) there was a stampeded
   (c) they were calm and orderly
   (d) there were fights

5. Where were people spending their nights in Tokyo?
   (a) offices
   (b) trains
   (c) homes
   (d) rescue centres

II. Read the news article and answer the questions that follow.

India beat Sri Lanka to win ICC World Cup 2011

MUMBAI, APRIL 2, 2011: An inspired India on Saturday night regained the coveted World Cup after 28 years as they suppressed Sri Lanka with a six-wicket victory in a nerve-wrecking final to script a glorious new chapter in their cricketing history.

Chasing 275 for a historic win, the Indians held their nerves as they rode on Gautam Gambhir's 97 and Mahendra Singh Dhoni's unbeaten 91 to overhaul the target with 10 balls to spare and send the cricket-crazy nation into frenzy.

The vociferous, jam-packed crowd at the Wankhede stadium erupted in wild celebrations as Dhoni hit the winning six runs to give India their biggest cricketing moment and crown themselves the ODI world champions, in addition to being the number one Test team

The World Cup title triumph, coming as it did after more than two decades, was doubly special for Sachin Tendulkar since it was the only silverware missing from his collection. It was also a fitting farewell to coach Gary Kirsten, for whom it was the last day in office as the Indian coach. The players, many of them with tears in their eyes, rushed to the ground to hug each other as Dhoni finished it off in style by hitting a six, as fire crackers lit up the evening sky to mark the moment.

1. When was the last time India won the World Cup?
   (a) 1986 (b) 2000
   (c) 1983 (d) 1999
2. How many runs did Mahendra Singh Dhoni score?
   (a) 91 (b) 97
   (c) 100 (d) 95
3. Who scored the winning run?
   (a) Gautam Gambhir
   (b) Mahendra Singh Dhoni
   (c) Sachin Tendulkar
   (d) Gary Kirsten
4. As used in the passage, what does the word 'silverware' mean?
   (a) silver coins
   (b) a new car model
   (c) cutlery
   (d) trophy
5. Who had his farewell on the same day?
   (a) Sachin Tendulkar
   (b) Mahendra Singh Dhoni
   (c) Sourav Ganguly
   (d) Gary Kirsten

III. Read the news article and answer the questions that follow.

Onion Prices to Rise Further

MUMBAI, 24 AUGUST 2015: Onion prices, which are already ruling at around Rs 80 per kg in most parts of the country, are likely to increase further by 10 per cent on tight supplies due to unseasonal rains affecting the crops.

"The situation is going to be more critical in future and we expect the price will go up by another 10 per cent in the coming days because the current crop, which is expected to hit the market next month, might be affected due to scanty rainfall," Bombay APMC Director Ashok Valu.

Onions imported from Pakistan are already in the market and the lot from Egypt would hit the market next week, he said, but added that this would not help much in bringing down the prices.

"The 100-200 containers, 30 tonne each, of onions imported will be distributed in the entire country. Mumbai itself needs 80-100 trucks daily, each containing 12 tonnes. Moreover, our domestic stock is also depleting fast. So imports will not be able to bring down the prices," he said.

The wholesale price of onion has risen to around Rs 60 per kg at Lasalgaon in Maharashtra while it is already selling at around Rs 80 per kg in retail markets.

About 700 kg of onion worth Rs 50,000 was allegedly stolen from a shop in suburban Mumbai, the police said yesterday. In Nashik, a farmer complained to the Nandgaon police that about 2,000 kgs of onion was stolen from his place. Despite the government taking measures, prices have gone up unabated both in the wholesale and retail markets across the country in the last few weeks due to tight supply following shortfall in the domestic output.

1. What has affected the onion production?
    (a) scanty rainfall
    (b) theft from godowns
    (c) pesticides
    (d) farmer suicides
2. Onions have been imported from which two countries?
    (a) Egypt and Sudan
    (b) Bangladesh and Pakistan
    (c) Afghanistan and Pakistan
    (d) Pakistan and Egypt
3. How much onion does Mumbai need on a daily basis?
    (a) 80–100 trucks each containing 12 tonnes
    (b) 12 tonnes
    (c) 700 kg
    (d) 2,000 kg
4. What is the price of onion at Lasalgaon?
    (a) Rs 80 kg   (b) Rs 60 kg
    (c) Rs 100 kg   (d) Rs 90 kg
5. As used in the passage, what does the word 'unabated' mean?
    (a) without becoming less
    (b) decreasing order
    (c) diminishing monsoon
    (d) shortage

BROCHURES

IV. Read the brochure and answer the questions that follow.

Want to be a reporter?

Do you like to conduct interviews? Do you find gathering information exciting? Are you up for some real-life action? Here's your chance to do all of these things. A leading English newspaper is looking for reporters.

Key responsibilities
- Tracking latest news stories.
- Collecting information on current events.
- Investigating/finding interesting and important news pieces.
- Preparing reports that are factually verified.
- Interviewing personalities as and when required.

Abilities required
- Should have a "nose for news".
- Should have excellent communication skills.
- Must be able to interact with people.
- Must be observant with great listening skills.
- Responsible.
- Keen to uncover the truth and does not meddle facts with false information.

Qualifications required
- A degree in journalism or mass communication.
- Prior experience in the same field will also count.

Warning
There will be distractions, tight deadlines and stress-filled days. May have to forgo weekends and holidays.

1. Who is looking for reporters?
    (a) a TV channel (b) a newspaper
    (c) a radio channel (d) a magazine
2. Which of these words is a synonym of the word 'reporter'?
    (a) journalist
    (b) author
    (c) anchor
    (d) private investigator
3. Taking up this job might mean giving up on _____
    (a) junk food
    (b) watching TV
    (c) weekends
    (d) hanging out with friends
4. What are two essential skills for this job?
    (a) reading and writing
    (b) driving and cooking
    (c) singing and dancing
    (d) communication and listening
5. What are the qualifications required for this job?
    (a) Journalism and Mass comm.
    (b) Masters degree in Physics
    (c) Bachelor of Science
    (d) Engineering

V. Read the brochure and answer the questions that follow.

Yoga Classes for Kids and Teenagers
15th September – 14th October
Age 6-11 years Time 4.15 pm-5.30 pm
Age 12-16 years Time 6 pm-7.15 pm
Price: Rs 3,000 per person

Your kids will have an opportunity to:
- Understand the importance of mental and physical health.
- Develop flexibility, strength, stamina, agility, balance and coordination.
- Learn the importance of good posture.
- Focus on internal welfare and relaxation.
- Feel positive and cope better with stress.
- Increase concentration, self-discipline and inner strength.
- Build self-confidence, motivation and persistence to achieve goals.

To book a seat call:
999999999
Or email: yogaclasses@yoga.com
Address: House no. 1215
Greater Kailash
Z, block
New Delhi

1. What is the duration of the course?
   (a) a week
   (b) a month
   (c) two weeks
   (d) three weeks
2. What is the timing of the class for teenagers?
   (a) 4.15 – 5.30 pm
   (b) 7.30 – 8 pm
   (c) 5.30 – 6.45 pm
   (d) 6.00 – 7.15 pm
3. What is the meaning of the word 'agility'?
   (a) to be able to move quickly
   (b) to be able to sleep better
   (c) to be able to fight illnesses
   (d) to be very strong
4. What is the duration of the classes?
   (a) one hour
   (b) one hour and fifteen minutes
   (c) two hours
   (d) one and the half hour
5. Which of these things can NOT be learned at these classes?
   (a) relaxation technique
   (b) cooking healthy food
   (c) self-discipline
   (d) good posture

LETTERS

VI. Read the letter and answer the questions that follow.

Dear Mom and Dad,

I'm enjoying my holidays at Grandma's home in Kolkata. I am in love with the city and don't intend to come back for a while.

Kolkata is a huge city and is always bustling with life. Someone had rightly named it the "city of joy". The streets are always filled with people from all races of life. In fact you will spot numerous travellers, like me, walking past its colonial monuments and enjoying the rich culture of the city.

There are museums, planetariums, libraries, cricket grounds and football stadiums, amusement parks and what not – each telling its own story from the past. I have already covered quite a few of these attractions. I visited the Nicco Park, the huge amusement park, which is often referred to as the Disneyland of Kolkata. I watched a starry show at the Birla Planetarium, which is the largest of its kind in Asia and the second largest in the world. I paid a visit to the Science Museum and the Botanical Gardens as well. The Botanical Gardens houses some 12,000 trees! Today, Grandma and I are going to visit the Alipore Zoo. Grandma was saying the zoo displays a large number of animals including the Royal Bengal Tiger, African Lion, jaguar, hippopotamus, Great Indian One-Horned Rhinoceros, Reticulated Giraffe, Grant's Zebra, Emu, Dromedary Camel and Indian Elephant. It is also a great picnic spot. It's very hot in Kolkata. Grandma and I often spend the afternoons eating ice lollies. Grandma cooks me a lot of good food. In the evenings we take Sasha to the park. Sasha likes running and playing with a ball. I throw the ball. Sasha runs after it and brings it back to me. The children in the park love Sasha.

Grandma sends her love. I will write back soon again.

Love,

Bikash

1. What is the other name for Kolkata that the letter mentions?
   (a) City of joy
   (b) City of dreams
   (c) City of pleasure
   (d) City of tourists
2. What kind of a place is Nicco Park?
   (a) Planetarium
   (b) Museum
   (c) Amusement park
   (d) Zoological garden
3. How many trees are there at the Botanical Gardens?
   (a) 10,000
   (b) 12,000
   (c) 1,200
   (d) 1,20,000
4. Which of these animals will not be found in the Alipore Zoo?
   (a) Indian Elephant
   (b) African Lion
   (c) Royal Bengal Tiger
   (d) Emperor Penguin
5. Which of these places in Kolkata has Bikash NOT visited?
   (a) Birla Planetarium
   (b) Victoria Memorial
   (c) Botanical Gardens
   (d) Nicco Park
6. Who do you think Sasha is?
   (a) Bikash's cousin
   (b) Grandma's dog
   (c) Grandfather
   (d) Grandma's bird

VII. Read the letter and answer the questions that follow.

26 June 2015
Mrs. and Mr. Jain
15 Park Avenue
Lower Parel
Mumbai
McDonalds
South City Mall
Mumbai

Dear Manager,

I am writing to complain about the terrible service me and my family received in your South City Mall branch last week.

My family and I entered your restaurant hoping to grab a quick bite before a movie show we were going to watch that day. We joined the queue as soon as we entered.

We waited for what seemed like hours only to be served by a grumpy-looking waiter, who was not only rude but also got our order completely wrong. We are vegetarians and were shocked to find chicken pieces in our burgers. When we tried to report it and get the right burgers, the waiter there said that we placed the wrong order and would have to pay again to get vegetarian burgers. This is absolutely untrue – why would we order chicken for vegetarians?

My kids were really hungry, so I had no choice but to reorder, and waited even longer. Consequently, we missed the first 45 minutes of our movie.

I am enclosing the receipts and I expect a full refund of our disastrous meal. I await your reply within the next seven days.

Yours Sincerely,

Mr. and Mrs. Jain

1. Who among the Jains has written this letter?
   (a) the parents
   (b) the daughter
   (c) the son
   (d) a lawyer they hired
2. What were the Jains going to do that day after their meal?
   (a) go for bowling
   (b) watch a cricket match
   (c) attend a party
   (d) watch a movie
3. What kind diet do the Jains follow?
   (a) fruitarian
   (b) gluten-free
   (c) vegetarian
   (d) low-calorie
4. Why did they choose to reorder?
   (a) they had a lot of time
   (b) they children were hungry
   (c) they love the restaurant food
   (d) the waiter forced them to
5. Why have the Jains written this letter?
   (a) to ask for a refund
   (b) to ask for apology
   (c) to ask for free burgers
   (d) to ask for free movie tickets

VIII. Read the letter and answer the questions that follow.

Vishaka Roy
Principal
Joseph Valley School
Chennai

Mr Mundhra
Bandiram's Snack Corner
Old Madras Road
Chennai

Dear Mr Mundhra,

Let me begin by thanking you for your past contributions to our school. Your sponsorship during our annual fests aided in the purchase of ten computers and several pieces of laboratory equipment for higher classes.

Next month, our school is organizing a teachers' get-together. We are planning to have a breakfast honouring retired teachers for their past years of service and present teachers for all the hard work they put in making our school of the top ones in the country.

We would like to place an order with your company for lavish buffet serving all kinds of Indian breakfast choices. It would be for 50 individuals. We would also require tea and coffee services. We hope you will be able to take up this order, even though it comes at a very short notice.

As you are a committed sponsor and long-time associate, we hope that you will be able to join us for breakfast as well.

Respectfully Yours,
Vishaka Roy

1. What was the school able to buy with Bandiram's sponsorship money?
   (a) ten blackboards
   (b) ten computers and equipments for laboratory
   (c) ten desks
   (d) ten books
2. Why is the school organizing the teacher's get-together?
   (a) to thank teachers for their hard work
   (b) to bid farewell to a teacher
   (c) to celebrate teacher's day
   (d) to welcome a new teacher
3. When is the get-together going to be held?
   (a) afternoon   (b) evening
   (c) late night   (d) morning
4. Who is the author of this letter?
   (a) a student of the school
   (b) a parent of a student
   (c) principal of the school
   (d) a teacher
5. Apart from the teachers, who else has been invited to the breakfast?
   (a) students   (b) parents
   (c) Mr Mundhra   (d) Mrs Roy

Reading Comprehension - II

NEWS REPORTS

I. **Read these news reports and answer the questions that follow.**

1. Fake cops who conned women, senior citizens held in Mira Road.
   (i) According to this report, what happened to the women and senior citizens?
      (a) someone cheated them and stole money.
      (b) someone kidnapped them.
      (c) someone misbehaved with them.
      (d) someone kidnapped their relatives.
   (ii) What do you understand by the term 'fake cops'?
      (a) senior policemen
      (b) traffic policemen
      (c) people pretending to be police
      (d) policemen
   (iii) How have the fake cops been punished?
      (a) they have been lathi charged.
      (b) they are not being allowed to leave a certain place
      (c) they have been tied with ropes.
      (d) they have been arrested.

2. Jharkhand boy makes acting debut in the latest Spider-Man film.
   (i) According to this report, who has made an acting debut?
      (a) a boy named Jharkhand.
      (b) a boy from Jharkhand.
      (c) a boy whose family name is Jharkhand.
      (d) a boy whose father's name is Jharkhand.
   (ii) What does the word debut mean?
      (a) doing something better than the others.
      (b) doing something someone likes
      (c) doing something for the first time.
      (d) doing something on a daily basis.

3. Despite drizzle, Mumbai continues to sizzle at 39 degrees Celsius.
   (i) What is the weather like in Mumbai?
      (a) it is breezy
      (b) it is stormy
      (c) it is very cold
      (d) it is very hot
   (ii) According to the report, the weather condition did not change even after
      (a) some rain
      (b) some cold days
      (c) people using sunscreen lotion.
      (d) people using umbrellas.

4. Swine flu claims one more life in Jamnagar.
   (i) What has happened according to the report?
      (a) only one person died of swine flu.
      (b) a person is suffering from swine flu.
      (c) a person claims he has swine flu.
      (d) one more person has died of swine flu.

5. Glaring short comings noticed in tiger sanctuaries.
   (i) What has been noticed in the sanctuaries?
      (a) short visits by tourists
      (b) flashing lights
      (c) flaw in its running
      (d) tigers running away for short periods
   (ii) What do you understand by the word sanctuary?
      (a) an open forest
      (b) a zoo with animals in cages
      (c) a protective natural environment
      (d) an animal hospital

6. Ancient sculptures find place amidst rubble.
   According to this report, what has happened to ancient sculptures?
   (a) they have been destroyed.
   (b) they have been shifted to a new museum.
   (c) they have been stolen.
   (d) they are lying with broken, discarded stuff.
7. Public cry foul over dump yard.
   According to the report, what is the public's reaction?
   (a) they think the dumpyard is actually something else.
   (b) they are upset because of the bad smell.
   (c) they are upset because birds are dying.
   (d) they are protesting against some wrong doing.
8. After 6 years, runaway Rajsamand boy came back home from Andhra.
   What happened 6 years ago?
   (a) the boy in question had been kidnapped.
   (b) the boy in question ran away from home.
   (c) the boy in question ran a marathon.
   (d) the boy in question ran in Olympics.

BIOGRAPHIES & SHORT NARRATIVES

II. Read the passage and answer the questions that follow.

Mother Teresa was born in 1910, in Skopje, capital of the Republic of Macedonia. Little is known about her early life, but at a young age she felt a calling to be a nun and serve through helping the poor. At the age of 18 she was given permission to join a group of nuns in Ireland. After a few months of training, with the Sisters of Loreto, she was then given permission to travel to India. She took her formal religious vows in 1931. On her arrival in India, she began by working as a teacher, however the widespread poverty of Calcutta made a deep impression on her; and this led to her starting a new order called "The Missionaries of Charity". The primary objective of this mission was to look after people, who nobody else was prepared to look after.

In 1948, she left the convent to live full time amongst the poorest of Calcutta. For many years, Mother Teresa and a small band of fellow nuns survived on minimal income and food, often having to beg for funds. But, slowly her efforts with the poorest were noted and appreciated by the local community and Indian politicians.

Over time the work grew. Missions were started overseas, and by 2013, there are 700 missions operating in over 130 countries. The scope of their work also expanded to include orphanages and hospices for those with terminal illness.

In 1979, she was awarded the Nobel Peace Prize "for work undertaken in the struggle to overcome poverty and distress, which also constitutes a threat to peace." She didn't attend the ceremonial banquet, but asked that the $192,000 fund be given to the poor.

Over the last two decades of her life, Mother Teresa suffered various health problems but nothing could dissuade her from fulfilling her mission of serving the poor and needy. Until her very last illness, she was active in travelling around the world to the different branches of "The Missionaries of Charity". She passed away on 5 September, 1997.

1. When she was 18, Mother Teresa joined a group of nuns in?
   (a) England (b) Ireland
   (c) Kolkata (d) Mumbai
2. When did Mother Teresa take her religious vows?
   (a) 1931 (b) 1932
   (c) 1933 (d) 1934
3. Mother Teresa was awarded the Nobel Prize in 1979. What was it for?
   (a) Power   (b) Physics
   (c) Peace   (d) Poverty

4. What is the name of the mission started by Mother Teresa?
   (a) Missionaries of Poverty
   (b) Missionaries of Charity
   (c) Sisters of Loreto
   (d) Republic of Macedonia

5. Where was Mother Teresa born?
   (a) Skejpo
   (b) Sojpe
   (c) Skojpe
   (d) Skopje

III. Read the passage and answer the questions that follow.

One of the earliest urban civilizations in India and in fact, in the world, was the Indus Valley Civilization, also called the Harappan Culture.

About 5,000 years ago, a group of nomads travelling from Sumeria (present-day Iran) entered North Western India, near present day Karachi. These nomads found a land so richly fertile by the banks of the river Indus that they settled there without hesitation. This area was abundant with water, fodder and fuel. Over the next thousand years, the immigrants spread over an area of half a million square miles. Excavations prove that the level of urban planning and architecture prevalent here was incomparable. The anchor for this civilization lay in the beautiful twin cities of Mohenjo-Daro and Harappa. The name Mohenjo-Daro means 'Mound of the Dead' in Sindhi. The city was built around 2600 BC and abandoned around 1700 BC. Evidence suggests that the city was highly prone to floods.

These cities were made of bricks – either baked mud of wood bricks. The amazing part was that the workers made every brick of the same size.

Despite a population of about 30,000, the city had one of the best sanitation systems. Each house had a well from which it drew water. From a bathing room the waste water was directed into covered drains along the main streets. Since all the streets were well-drained, the city remained dry and clean. This is the evidence of a very modern method of sanitation and sewerage. Houses were well protected from noise, odour and thieves. Each house opened out onto inner courtyards and smaller lanes, so it was safe. Although some houses were larger than the others, the city seemed to promote an equal society, for all houses had the same kind of access to water and drainage. The city had an impressive defense structure in place as well. Though it lacked outer walls, there were defensive towers in the West and South.

1. What is also referred to as the Harappan Culture?
   (a) Mohenjo-Daro
   (b) Iran
   (c) Karachi
   (d) Indus Valley Civilization

2. Why did people readily settle in the Indus Valley?
   (a) The land was very fertile
   (b) There were houses already constructed
   (c) There was the best sanitation system
   (d) The area was well-protected

3. The word 'Mohenjo-Daro' is in which language?
   (a) Hindi   (b) Parsee
   (c) Sindhi   (d) Punjabi

4. What was the name of Iran in earlier times?
   (a) Sumeria
   (b) Karachi
   (c) Mohenjo-Daro
   (d) Sumatra

5. What was the best in the twin cities?
   (a) Education system
   (b) Political system
   (c) Policing
   (d) Sanitation system

6. The Indus Valley civilization derives its name from a _____
   (a) River
   (b) Another city
   (c) Tribe
   (d) Mountain

Reading Comprehension - II

IV. Read the passage and answer the questions that follow.

One of the most powerful emperors of India, Ashoka's life was a journey from a power-hungry, merciless ruler to a believer in ahimsa, or non-violence.

Ashoka (304-232 BCE) was born to Mauryan Emperor Bindusara and Maharani Dharma. His grandfather, Chandragupta Maurya was the founder of the Mauryan Empire. Right from his childhood days, Ashoka showed a great skill in handling weapons and had a keen interest in warfare. Ashoka had many brothers who wanted to take the throne after their father's death, but Ashoka fought and killed them all to become the King of Magadha, in present-day Bihar. After becoming the King, Ashoka fought many wars to expand his empire. He was a ruthless ruler, ready to do anything to conquer. Ashoka's reign of terror continued for eight long years, earning him the name "Chandashok". At the peak of his kingship, his empire stretched from the Hindu Kush Mountains in Afghanistan in the north-west to present-day Bangladesh and Assam in the east, and to parts of Tamil Nadu and Andhra Pradesh in the south. He fought his last battle at Kalinga, in present-day Odisha, which proved to be the turning point in his life. This fierce battle made him realize the terrible consequences of war. More than 10,000 people had lost their lives in the Kalinga War. Saddened by the sufferings of the defeated people, Ashoka vowed to give up war and adopt the path of peace shown by Gautam Buddha. He made Buddhism his state religion and helped spread its messages around the world, sending envoys as far as ancient Rome and Egypt. He sent his son, Mahindra, and daughter, Sanghamitra, to Ceylon (now Sri Lanka) to spread Buddhist ideas.

1. Who was the founder of the Mauryan Empire?
   (a) Ashoka
   (b) Bindusara
   (c) Chandragupta Maurya
   (d) Maharani Dharma

2. If you had to go to Magadha today, which Indian state would you head to?
   (a) Odisha   (b) Sri Lanka
   (c) Tamil Nadu (d) Bihar

3. Where did Ashoka fight his last battle?
   (a) Kalinga   (b) Magadha
   (c) Kush Mountains (d) Andhra Pradesh

4. Ashoka became the ambassador of which religion?
   (a) Jainism
   (b) Hinduism
   (c) Buddhism
   (d) Islam

5. Why was Ashoka given the title of 'Chandashok'?
   (a) because he gave up war
   (b) because he was merciless
   (c) because he was strong
   (d) because he was the grandson of Chandragupta

V. Read the passage and answer the questions that follow.

The Solar System is made-up of the Sun and all of the smaller objects that move around it. Apart from the Sun, the large members of the Solar System are the eight major planets. Nearest the Sun are four fairly small, rocky planets - Mercury, Venus, Earth and Mars.

Beyond Mars is the asteroid belt – a region populated by millions of rocky objects. These are leftovers from the formation of the planets, 4.5 billion years ago.

On the far side of the asteroid belt are the four gas giants - Jupiter, Saturn, Uranus and Neptune. These planets are much bigger than Earth, but they are of very lightweight for their size. They are mostly made of hydrogen and helium.

Until recently, the furthest known planet was an icy world called Pluto. However, Pluto is dwarfed by Earth's Moon and many astronomers think it is too small to be called a true planet. An object named Eris, which is at least as big as Pluto, was discovered very far from the Sun in 2005. More than 1,000 icy worlds such as Eris have been discovered beyond Pluto in recent years. These are called Kuiper Belt Objects. In 2006, the International Astronomical Union decided that Pluto and Eris must be classed as "dwarf planets".

Even further out are the comets of the OortCloud. These are so far away that they are invisible in even the largest telescopes. Every so often one of these comets is disturbed and Heads towards the Sun. It then becomes visible in the night sky.

1. Which of these is a rocky planet?
   (a) Jupiter (b) Mercury
   (c) Saturn   (d) Uranus
2. Which of these is a gas giant?
   (a) Neptune (b) Venus
   (c) Earth   (d) Mars
3. Pluto has been classified as a dwarf planet? Name another dwarf planet.
   (a) Iris   (b) Ires
   (c) Eros   (d) Eris
4. Which of these is not bigger than the Earth?
   (a) Jupiter
   (b) Saturn
   (c) Mercury
   (d) Uranus
5. What kind of objects are there in the Asteroid Belt?
   (a) gassy   (b) rocky
   (c) sandy   (d) dusty

NOTICES

VI. Read the notice and answer the questions that follow.

Indira Community
Neighbourhood Organization Meeting
Sunday, 30 August, 2015
12:30 pm at the Indira Club House

The Homeowner's Association is organizing a meeting to discuss the neighbourhood safety issues. All the members are requested to be present and raise any concerns or questions they may have. As suggested by some member parents, the idea of building an enclosed play area for the kids of the neighbourhood will also be discussed with the builders. We look forward to seeing you there.

Yours truly,

Md. Khan (Secretary)

1. Where will the meeting be held?
   (a) Indira Community
   (b) Indira Clubhouse
   (c) Indira Conference Room
   (d) Indira Meeting Hall
2. Which of these statements is true?
   (a) The meeting will be held on a Saturday
   (b) The meeting will be held on 31 August
   (c) The meeting will be held at 12.30 pm
   (d) The meeting will be held at Indira Community
3. Who is the organizer of the meeting?
   (a) Homeowner's Association
   (b) Indira Community
   (c) Neighbourhood Organization
   (d) Md. Khan

SECTION 3
SPOKEN AND WRITTEN EXPRESSIONS

Spoken and Written Expressions

Asking for permission, making a request appropriately, refusing to do something you don't want to and saying sorry for a wrongdoing: all of these can be done in a variety of ways. Let's take a look at how to express our feelings and thoughts in a right way.

Making Requests
It is important to be polite when we request for something. Here are some ways of making a request.
- Can you show me your photo album, please?
  Yes, of course.
- Will you lend me your book, please?
  Yes, sure.
- Could you please show me the way to the post office?
  Certainly.
- Would you help me with this exercise, please?
  Sure.
- Would you mind lending me your pen, please?
  No, not at all.

> Remember, 'could' is more polite than saying 'can'.

Making Refusals
Sometimes people ask us to do things which we don't like or don't want to do. It is important to speak and say 'No'. Here are some ways to do so.
- Strong refusals
  (i) No way.
  (ii) Absolutely not.
  (iii) No chance.
- Almost certain refusals
  (i) Not likely.
  (ii) I don't want to.
- Polite refusals
  (i) I'd rather not.
  (ii) No but thanks for asking.

How to Apologise
To apologize is to tell someone that you are sorry for having done something that has caused them inconvenience or unhappiness.

Here are some expressions that we can use to make an apology.
- I apologise
- I must apologise for...
- I'd like to apologise for...
- I am so sorry for...
- I shouldn't have...
- Please, forgive me for...
- I'm terribly sorry for...
- Please, accept my apologies for...

We may use some of these expressions to accept an apology
- That's all right.
- Never mind.
- Don't apologise.
- It doesn't matter.
- Don't worry about it.
- That's okay.
- No harm done.

PRACTICE EXERCISE

Choose the correct option to make appropriate requests, refusals and apologies in the following situations.

1. You are writing an exam. The only pen you carried with you has stopped working. (Request)
   (a) Could I borrow a pen, please?
   (b) Give me your pen.
   (c) Pen please!
   (d) I need a pen.

2. Your teacher accuses you of cheating during the exam. You know you didn't. (Refuse politely)
   (a) I'm sorry, but there has been a misunderstanding.
   (b) No way.
   (c) No but thanks for asking.
   (d) Are you out of your mind?

3. You forgot to return the pen you borrowed from your friend. Now you have lost it. (Apologize)
   (a) I lost your pen.
   (b) I already returned your pen, you must have forgotten.
   (c) I'm so sorry I lost your pen.
   (d) Never mind.

4. You lost your friend's pen. You apologize to him and he readily forgives you. He says _____. (Accept apology)
   (a) Get out of my sight.
   (b) You should be sorry.
   (c) Thanks for losing my pen.
   (d) That's all right.

5. You are in the store and your friend asks you to help steal something. You don't approve. (Refuse strongly)
   (a) Sure.
   (b) Absolutely not.
   (c) I'll think about it.
   (d) Of course.

6. Your car broke down and you need to go to work. You see your neighbour, who goes the same way just starting for work. (Request)
   (a) I'm coming with you.
   (b) Drive fast!
   (c) If you don't mind, could I come with you?
   (d) Let's go!

7. You enter office in a hurry and while walking past someone's desk, you accidentally drop some papers off his desk. (Apologize formally)
   (a) I'm terribly sorry, I should have watched my step.
   (b) Please pick those up.
   (c) You were on my way.
   (d) I'm in a rush.

8. You are a restaurant manager. A guest is smoking inside the restaurant and he is not supposed to. While asking him to stop you must make sure he is not offended. (Request, formal)
   (a) Stop smoking immediately!
   (b) If you don't mind Sir, could you please stop smoking?
   (c) If you don't mind Sir, could you leave?
   (d) Don't you know Sir you are not supposed to smoke here?

9. You were playing with your brother's favourite toy and you broke it. (Apologize informally)
   (a) Not that you paid for it.
   (b) You gave me a broken toy.
   (c) I'll get you a new toy.
   (d) I'm sorry I wasn't careful.

10. A friend invites you to a party. You can't make it. (Refuse politely)
    (a) No way!
    (b) Absolutely not!
    (c) No, but thanks for inviting me.
    (d) Please don't invite me.

11. You have guests over. They love the desert you made. You want to offer them a second helping. (Request)
    (a) Serve yourselves.
    (b) Please help yourselves.
    (c) The cake's on the table.
    (d) Would you like some more cake?

12. You were angry and you called someone a name. You realize your fault later. (Apologize)
    (a) I shouldn't have said that.
    (b) You deserve it.
    (c) I can't control my anger.
    (d) Calm down.
13. A neighbour who is going on a vacation asks you to feed his dog. You cannot do this. (Refuse politely)
    (a) I hate dogs.
    (b) I'm afraid it won't be possible.
    (c) Leave me alone.
    (d) Never!
14. A friend wants to copy your homework. You worked hard on it and do not like the idea. (Strong refusal)
    (a) I'd rather you didn't.
    (b) Sure.
    (c) No chance.
    (d) Go ahead!
15. You are leaving office in a hurry so that you don't miss your doctor's appointment. A colleague wants to talk. (Refuse politely)
    (a) Get out of my way.
    (b) I'm afraid I have to leave.
    (c) What's up?
    (d) No, I don't want to talk.
16. The food you ordered at a restaurant is cold. You call the waiter. (Request)
    (a) Could you take this back and serve it hot?
    (b) You shouldn't have served cold food.
    (c) Why is the food cold, could you explain?
    (d) I can't eat this.
17. You borrowed your sister's dress and got a stain on it. (Apologize informally)
    (a) I'm sorry I got your dress stained.
    (b) Please forgive me for my sins.
    (c) I seek your forgiveness.
    (d) I made a mistake, but that's okay.
18. You needed a pencil, and you took a classmate's without asking. (Apologize formally)
    (a) Here's your pencil, sorry.
    (b) I took your pencil, hope it's all right.
    (c) Sorry, I needed the pencil.
    (d) I wanted to apologize for taking this without your permission.
19. A wife wants her husband to do some grocery shopping on his way back home. (Request)
    (a) Could you get some grocery on your way back?
    (b) Get some grocery on your way back.
    (c) Don't forget the grocery please!
    (d) Are you going to get the grocery or not?
20. Your father asked you to post a letter but you lost it on the way. (Apologize formally)
    (a) I'm terribly sorry, I lost the letter.
    (b) Could you write the letter again, please?
    (c) I don't know where I kept the letter.
    (d) I can't find the letters.

SECTION 4
ACHIEVERS' SECTION

Some Thoughtful Questions

1. Match items in List A with their meanings in List B.

A	B
wounded	got up from sleep
awoke	give back
forgive	small patches of ground for plants
faithful	severely injured
pity	Pardon
beds	Loyal
return	feel sorry for

Use any three of the above words in sentences of your own. You may change the form of the word.

Answer:

A	B
wounded	severely injured
awoke	got up from sleep
forgive	pardon
faithful	loyal
pity	feel sorry for
beds	small patches of ground for plants
return	give back

Sentences with three words:
1. Pallavi had to return the bag to her friend.
2. One should be faithful to one's friends.
3. The dreadful dream awoke Reshma from sleep.

2. **Complete the following word ladder with the help of the clues given below.**

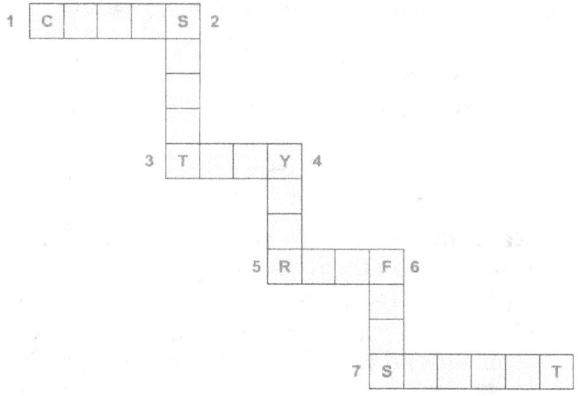

1. Mother will be very _____ if you don't go to school.
2. As soon as he caught _____ of the teacher, Mohan started writing.
3. How do you like my _____ kitchen garden? Big enough for you, is it?
4. My youngest sister is now a _____ old.
5. Standing on the _____, he saw children playing on the road.
6. Don't make such a _____. Nothing will happen.
7. Don't cross the _____ till the green light comes on.

Answer:

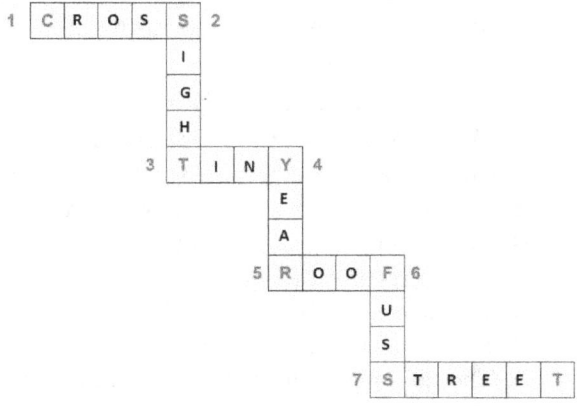

1. Mother will be very **cross** if you don't go to school.
2. As soon as he caught **sight** of the teacher, Mohan started writing.
3. How do you like my **tiny** kitchen garden? Big enough for you, is it?
4. My youngest sister is now a **year** old.
5. Standing on the **roof**, he saw children playing on the road.
6. Don't make such a **fuss**. Nothing will happen.
7. Don't cross the **street** till the green light comes on.

3. **Read the following paragraph and frame questions on the italicized phrases.**

   Anil is *in school*. I am in school too. Anil is sitting *in the left row*. He is reading a book. Anil's friend is sitting in the second row. He is *sharpening his pencil*. *The teacher* is writing on the blackboard. Children are writing in their copybooks. Some children are *looking out of the window*.

   _____
   _____
   _____
   _____
   _____
   _____

   Answer:
   1. Where is Anil?
   2. Which row is Anil sitting in?
   3. What is he doing?
   4. Which row is Anil's friend sitting in?
   5. What is his friend doing?
   6. Who is writing on the blackboard?
   7. What are some of the children doing?

4. **Based on the following points write a story.**
   ■ Your aunt has gone to her mother's house.
   ■ Your uncle does his cooking.
   ■ He is absent-minded.
   ■ He puts vegetables on the stove.
   ■ He begins to clean his bicycle outside.
   ■ The neighbor calls out saying something is burning.
   ■ Your uncle rushes to the kitchen.
   ■ To save vegetables, he puts some oil on them.
   ■ Unfortunately, it's machine oil, not cooking oil.
   ■ What do you think happens to the vegetables?

   Begin like this:

   Last month my aunt decided to visit her parents…

   Answer:

   Last month my aunt decided to visit her parents. My uncle was alone at home, and so he used to cook for himself. He was a little absent-minded. Once it so happened that he put vegetables on the stove and went outside to clean his bicycle. After some time, the neighbour called him out, saying that something was burning. Uncle rushed inside. To save the vegetables, he put some oil on them. Unfortunately, it was machine oil and not cooking oil. The vegetables were not fit to be eaten now. Uncle had to throw it all away.

5. **Match items in Column A with those in Column B.**

A	B
(i) fuel	Lighted matchstick
(ii) oxygen	Air
(iii) heat	Coal
	Burning coal
	Wood
	Smouldering paper
	Cooking gas

   Answer:

A	B
(i) fuel	Smouldering paper
	Cooking gas
	Coal
	Wood
(ii) oxygen	Air
(iii) heat	Lighted matchstick
	Burning coal

6. **Write two paragraphs describing a bus ride to watch a cricket match in a village. Use the following points. Add some of your own.**
   - two-hour journey by bus
   - an old and crowded bus
   - friendly passengers
   - visit to a village fair where the match is to be played
   - the match between two village teams
   - makeshift stumps, rough pitch and a rubber ball
   - the match was enjoyable, but the trip was tiring

   Answer:

   Last weekend, I went on a trip to watch a cricket match in a village. It was a two-hour journey by bus. I was quite excited about the match. It was the first time I was going to be in a live audience. The bus was an old and crowded one, but the passengers were friendly.

   It was a visit to a village fair where the cricket match was to be played. The match was to be fought between two village teams. The accessories were makeshift stumps, a rubber ball, bat, etc. The pitch was quite rough. It was a great match. Both the teams played so well. We all enjoyed it thoroughly. We returned by night. The match was truly enjoyable, but the trip was tiring.

7. **What problems are you likely to face if you keep ants as pets? When a group of bees finds nectar, it informs other bees of its location, quantity, etc. through dancing. Can you guess what ants communicate to their fellow ants by touching one another's feelers?**

   Answer:

   There might be several problems if we keep ants as pets. They would start eating our food and other eatables. They bite. They won't listen to our orders. Ants communicate about food newly found by them to their fellow ants by touching one another's feelers.

8. **How do the smaller desert animals fulfil their need for water?**

   Answer:

   The smaller desert animals take various measures to fulfil their need for water:
   - Some of them burrow underground in the day time and come out only at night to eat.
   - Some others eat other animals and get the moisture from the meat.
   - Some eat plants and seeds and obtain plant juices.

9. **Describe a desert in your own way. Write a paragraph and read it aloud to your classmates.**

   Answer:

   A desert is a place which is hot and receives less rainfall. It is not entirely dry. Oasis is a green island in the desert where a well/spring gives water to the plants around. Camels can store water for a long time. Thus, they can survive in deserts for long. That's the reason the camel is called the ship of the desert.

10. **Do you think there is life on other planets? Can you guess what kind of people there may be on them? In what ways are they likely to be different from us?**

    Answer:

    We think there might be life on other planets. There is a lot of research to find out if there is life on other planets. Space scientists from various countries are continuously trying to search for any such evidence. Spacecraft have been sent to the moon and Mars.

    If there is any life form on other planets, that would be entirely different from us as they would have been exposed to different environmental conditions. They would have adapted accordingly.

Some Thoughtful Questions

Model Test Paper 1

I. Choose the correct option that identifies the noun in the following sentences.

1. My family and I went to the zoo yesterday.
    (a) and (b) family
    (c) went (d) to
2. Charlie Chaplin studied the art of clowning.
    (a) Charlie (b) art
    (c) studied (d) clowning
3. I saw a circus from China featuring a performer who spun many plates on sticks.
    (a) featuring (b) plates
    (c) China (d) performer
4. The accused refused to answer the question.
    (a) answer (b) refused
    (c) accused (d) the
5. The boy denied stealing the money.
    (a) denied (b) boy
    (c) stealing (d) the

II. Fill in the blanks with the correct article.

1. We usually have _____ dinner at eight
    (a) a (b) an
    (c) the (d) none of these
2. I'm against _____ capital punishment.
    (a) a (b) an
    (c) the (d) none of these
3. I bought _____ umbrella last week.
    (a) a (b) an
    (c) the (d) none of these
4. _____ roses are my favourite flowers.
    (a) a (b) an
    (c) the (d) none of these
5. His birthday is on _____ fourth of May.
    (a) a (b) the
    (c) an (d) none of these

III. Fill in the blanks with correct form of verb.

1. I _____ tennis every Sunday morning.
    (a) playing (b) play
    (c) am playing (d) am play
2. Don't make so much noise. Hari _____ to study for her ESL test.
    (a) try (b) tries
    (c) tried (d) is trying
3. It _____ many times every winter in Frankfurt.
    (a) snows (b) It snowed
    (c) It is snowing (d) It is snow
4. The phone _____. Can you answer it, please?
    (a) rings (b) ring
    (c) rang (d) is ringing
5. You can keep my iPod if you like. I _____ it any more.
    (a) don't use (b) doesn't use
    (c) didn't use (d) am not using

IV. Fill in the blanks with correct preposition.

1. I can not guess the answer _____ this question.
    (a) in (b) for
    (c) at (d) on
2. He is not known _____ my brother.
    (a) with (b) about
    (c) for (d) to
3. I am badly in need _____ money.
    (a) of (b) for
    (c) with (d) on
4. One should live _____ honest labours.
    (a) by (b) with
    (c) on (d) for
5. Rama was married _____ Sita.
    (a) by (b) to
    (c) with (d) for

V. Fill in the blanks with correct modal.

1. _____ I have more cheese on my sandwich?
    (a) Must (b) Could
    (c) Would (d) Have to
2. You _____ eat more vegetables.
    (a) should (b) might
    (c) may (d) could

3. I _____ like to buy the same television for my house.
   - (a) could
   - (b) must
   - (c) would
   - (d) have to
4. _____ I have a coffee please?
   - (a) must
   - (b) have to
   - (c) may
   - (d) would
5. We _____ go to the concert if the rain stops. We don't know for sure.
   - (a) mustn't
   - (b) might
   - (c) have to
   - (c) wouldn't

VI. Choose the correctly punctuated sentence.

1. Will your dad drive us to the museum or shall we take a bus?
   - (a) Will your dad drive us to the museum, or shall we take a bus?
   - (b) Will your dad, drive us to the museum, or shall we take a bus?
   - (c) Will your dad drive us to the museum or, shall we take a bus?
   - (d) None of these
2. After I had scraped the mud, off my shoes I went indoors.
   - (a) After I had scraped the mud off my shoes, I went indoors.
   - (b) After, I had scraped the mud off my shoes, I went indoors.
   - (c) After I had scraped the mud off my shoes, I went indoors.
   - (d) None of these
3. I have already read the book that you chose for your report
   - (a) I have already read, the book that you chose for your report.
   - (b) I have already read, the book that you chose, for your report.
   - (c) I have already read the book that you chose, for your report.
   - (d) I have already read the book that you chose for your report.
4. The principal entered the room and the students became silent
   - (a) The principal entered the room, and the students became silent.
   - (b) The principal, entered the room, and the students became silent.
   - (c) The principal entered the room, and the students, became silent.
   - (d) None of these
5. The car has low mileage, new tyres and rubber bumpers
   - (a) The car has low mileage, new tyres, and rubber bumpers.
   - (b) The car, has low mileage, new tyres, and rubber bumpers.
   - (c) The car has low mileage new tyres and rubber bumpers.
   - (d) None of these

VII. Choose the correct active/passive voice of the following sentences.

1. Someone has lit the fire.
   - (a) The fire was lit by someone.
   - (b) You are requested to light the fire by someone.
   - (c) The fire has been lit by someone.
   - (d) The fire had been lit by someone.
2. You surprise me.
   - (a) I am to be surprised.
   - (b) You surprised.
   - (c) I am surprised at you.
   - (d) He is surprised.
3. The boy killed the snake with a stick.
   - (a) The snake was killed by the boy with a stick.
   - (b) A stick was killed by the boys with a snake.
   - (c) A snake with stick was killed by the boy.
   - (d) A snake is killed by the boy with a stick.
4. Let me do this.
   - (a) Let us do this.
   - (b) This is to be done by me.
   - (c) Let this be done by me.
   - (d) Let I do this.

VIII. Choose the correct narration of the following sentences.

1. He remarked, "Two and two makes four."
   - (a) He remarked that two and two would make four.
   - (b) He remarked that two and two made four.
   - (c) He remarked that two and two makes four.
   - (d) He advised that two and two makes four.

Model Test Paper

2. Rahul said, "We must obey our parents."
   (a) Rahul remarked that we must obey our parents.
   (b) Rahul advised that we must obey our parents.
   (c) Rahul said that we must obey our parents.
   (d) Rahul said that we should obey our parents.

3. She said, "Madam, I have done my homework."
   (a) She said respectfully that she had been done homework.
   (b) She said respectfully that she has done her homework.
   (c) She told her madam that she had done her homework.
   (d) She said respectfully to her teacher that she had done her homework.

IX. **Read the following passages and answer the questions that follow.**

Teaching is the noblest of all professions. A teacher has a sacred duty to perform. It is he on whom rests the responsibility of moulding the character of young children. Apart from developing their intellect, he can inculcate in them qualities of good citizenship, remaining neat and clean, talking decently and sitting properly. These virtues are not so easy to imbibe. Only he who himself leads a life of simplicity, purity and rigid discipline can successfully cultivate these habits in his pupils.

Besides, a teacher always remains young. He may grow old in age but not in spite. Perpetual contact with budding youths keeps him happy and cheerful. There are moments when domestic worries weigh heavily on his mind, but the delightful company of innocent children makes him overcome his transient moods of despair.

Questions
1. What is the noblest of all professions?
   (a) Tailoring   (b) Teaching
   (c) Driving   (d) Cobbling

2. Who is responsible for shaping young characters?
   (a) Teacher   (b) Master
   (c) Engineer   (d) Doctor

3. Who inculcates good habits in whom?
   (a) Master   (b) Owner
   (c) Teacher   (d) Lord

4. How does a teacher lead a life?
   (a) Disciplined   (b) Ill mannered
   (c) Corrupt   (d) None of these

X. **Read the following passages and answer the questions that follow.**

There is a story of a man who thought he had a right to do what he liked. One day, this gentleman was walking along a busy road, spinning his walking-stick round and round in his hand, and was trying to look important. A man walking behind him objected.

"You ought not to spin your walking-stick round and round like that!" he said.

"I am free to do what I like with my walking-stick," argued the gentleman.

'Of course you are," said the other man, "but you ought to know that your freedom ends where my nose begins."

The story tells us that we can enjoy our rights and our freedom only when they do not interfere with other people's rights and freedom.

Questions
1. Why was the gentleman on the road moving his walking stick round and round?
2. Who objected him?
3. What argument did the gentleman give?
4. What did he say in reply?

Achievers' Section
Choose correct narration
1. The tiger caught a fox.
   (a) A fox has been caught by the tiger.
   (b) A fox was caught by the tiger.
   (c) A fox is caught by the tiger.
   (d) A fox had been caught by the tiger.

2. He said to me, "Do read the holy Gita daily."
   (a) He asked to me to read the holy Gita daily.
   (b) He asked me to do read the holy Gita daily.
   (c) He asked me to read the holy Gita daily.
   (d) He requested me to read the holy Gita daily.
3. He said, "May God bless you."
   (a) He wished that God bless him.
   (b) He prayed that may God bless him.
   (c) He told that may God bless him.
   (d) He wished that God might bless him.
4. Was the other man satisfied with argument? (Please see passage given in (X).
5. In whose company who remains young forever? (Please see passage given in (IX).
   (a) Bad children
   (b) Innocent children
   (c) Shy children
   (d) Rude children

Model Test Paper 2

SECTION-I : WORD AND STRUCTURE KNOWLEDGE

Choose the best word/phrase to complete each sentence.

1. This train is the only link _____ the village and the city.
   (a) from (b) for
   (c) between (d) to

2. If you don't know the meaning of a word, you can look it _____ in a dictionary.
   (a) for (b) up
   (c) down (d) to

3. He was _____ that he had failed his driving test.
   (a) Devastated (b) deviated
   (c) disgusted (d) derailed

4. If you act in haste, everything will go to waste. The word haste means _____.
   (a) Alone (b) selfishly
   (c) slowly (d) a hurry

5. He's had several arguments with his boss. The word argument can be replaced by _____.
   (a) fire ins (b) run ins
   (c) talk back (d) back into

6. People still have _____ doubts about his fitness.
   (a) — (b) much
   (c) lot of (d) any

7. We don't know what happened. We can only _____ on it.
   (a) Expect (b) detect
   (c) guesswork (d) speculate

8. I'm going to attend the talk by the noted economist Amartya Sen. 'Noted' means _____.
   (a) Famous (b) strict
   (c) intelligent (d) controversial

9. If I were a tiger, I _____ scare away all the people.
   (a) have to (b) would like to
   (c) like to (d) could able to

Choose the appropriate idiom.

10. He's doesn't like playing outdoors, he's an absolute _____.
    (a) couch head (b) sleepy head
    (c) bookworm (d) lazy tom

11. When he scored top marks, he was _____.
    (a) jumped out of his skin
    (b) on cloud and stars
    (c) high on joy
    (d) over the moon

Find where the error is in the sentence.

12. She walk / all the way / to school / everyday.
    (a) / (b) / (c) / (d)

13. We can't / reach school / lately or we / will be punished.
    (a) / (b) / (c) / (d)

14. The lady / within the black coat / is not / our headmistress.
    (a) / (b) / (c) / (d)

15. He studied / really hard / and performed really / goodly in the test.
    (a) / (b) / (c) / (d)

Choose the best option to complete each sentence.

16. The thief _____ through a hole in the fence to enter the garden.
    (a) crept   (b) bunged
    (c) swept   (d) crowed

17. A large _____ of whales was following the ship.
    (a) group   (b) class
    (c) school   (d) flock

18. We _____ completed all the remaining work for the school day.
    (a) have just   (b) had just
    (c) have just been   (d) had just been

19. The man had a nasty _____ running from his forehead to his cheek.
    (a) Mole   (b) scar
    (c) tear   (d) beard

20. He _____ his hands in several places as he fell.
    (a) pain   (b) ache
    (c) sore   (d) cut

Match the following sentences with the words below.

21. "Do you think you could type this out for me?" _____ _____.

22. "Men at work – take diversion." _____.

23. "Power switches – keep away." _____.

24. "Let's go to the beach." _____ _____.
    (a) A suggestion
    (b) A request
    (c) An announcement
    (d) An order

Choose the word that doesn't belong.

25. salad, ketchup, smoothie, custard
    (a) salad
    (b) ketchup
    (c) smoothie
    (d) custard

26. hop, sway, skip, jump
    (a) hop   (b) sway
    (c) skip   (d) jump

CHOOSE THE CORRECT ANSWER.

27. The senior _____ of this restaurant keeps all his recipes secret.
    (a) cooker   (b) cookie
    (c) chef   (d) chief

28. In India it is _____ to greet visitors with a Namaste.
    (a) customary   (b) ordinary
    (c) honorary   (d) preliminary

29. Limousines, casinos, yachts; he really lives his life _____.
    (a) on the high-flyer   (b) a real casanova
    (c) in the fast lane   (d) full of gizmos

30. Vinod _____ finish the race though he was tired.
    (a) could able to   (b) didn't able to
    (c) managed to   (d) was possible to

SECTION-II : READING

Read the passage and answer the questions that follow.

For some time now, I have been trying to decide who makes the world's best icecream. I have narrowed my list down to four manufacturers: Bobbins Naturals, Wall's, Wunderburst or Marshal. Let's start with Bobbins. They make very good ice cream. They have lots and lots of yummy flavours, but that's really not important - because I always get coffee flavour. They make the best coffee ice cream in the world. I've never drunk real hot coffee, but people tell me that Bobbins' coffee ice cream tastes just like the real thing. Besides, Bobbins uses all natural ingredients to make their ice cream which is a really good idea.

Second, there is Wall's. Wall's makes excellent ice cream. Like Bobbins, Wall's uses natural ingredients. But they only make three different flavours—strawberry, vanilla and choconut—but they make them really creamy and fruity. Especially the strawberry. Every bite of it reminds me of the strawberries that I used to eat at my gran's house. The vanilla flavour is wonderful. It is very smooth and has a fresh, creamy flavour. But the choconut flavour is the best. It is made with real cocoa beans from Columbia. I didn't know where Columbia is, so I looked for it on a map. I discovered that it is in South America! That's a long way to go to get cocoa, so it must be good. I would say that the only drawback to Wall's ice cream is that they only make three different flavours. Third, we have Wunderburst. Wunderburst ice cream is okay. They don't have many good flavours. Actually, the only Wunderburst flavour I like is Caramel. It is vanilla with little chunks of toffee in it. As you eat the ice cream, you can crunch through the toffee. That's pretty fun.

Finally, there is Marshal. Marshal ice cream is mediocre. The only good thing about Marshal is that it is relatively inexpensive. You can buy a whole carton of Marshal ice cream for ₹ 50.00. That's only my two-week allowance.

31. Which of the following would be the best title for this passage?
    (a) Strawberry, Vanilla, Choconut, and Toffee
    (b) The Four Top Ice Cream Manufacturers
    (c) The Finest Ice Cream in the World
    (d) Picking the Best Ice Cream Manufacturer

32. If the author wanted to get some coffee ice cream, where would he or she probably go?
    (a) Wunderburst
    (b) Bobbins
    (c) Marshal
    (d) Wall's

33. According to the passage, the author likes Bobbins ice cream because it _____.
    (a) is all natural
    (b) is made in Columbia
    (c) comes in toffee flavour
    (d) is mediocre

34. The author writes, "That's a long way to go to get cocoa, so it must be good." Using this information, we can understand that the author believes that _____.
    (a) Wall's is spending a lot of money on its ingredients
    (b) Columbia makes the best cocoa in the world
    (c) things that are hard to get must be high quality
    (d) cocoa from the other parts of the world is not very good

35. The author likes Wunderburst ice cream because it _____.
    (a) is relatively inexpensive
    (b) has coffee in it
    (c) is made in Columbia
    (d) is okay

36. According to the passage, how is Bobbins ice cream different from Wall's?
    (1) Bobbins has many different flavours and Wall's does not.
    (2) Bobbins uses all natural ingredients and Wall's does not.
    (3) Bobbins is very expensive and Wall's is not.
    (a) 1 only
    (b) 1 and 2 only
    (c) 2 and 3 only
    (d) 1, 2 and 3

37. Given the information in the passage, which of the following statements would the author mostlikely agree with?
    (a) Each manufacturer has its strengths and weaknesses.
    (b) The best manufacturers are the ones with the most flavours.
    (c) Manufacturers with fewer flavours are not usually popular.
    (d) Each manufacturer is good for different reasons.

Read the following list and answer the questions that follow.

- They bring you the menu and then become rare to find.
- They give you stale bread you didn't ask for and then charge you for it.
- They ignore you when you try to catch their eye.
- They give you mineral water when you want tap water and you pay through the nose for it.
- They serve you food that's outright bad, and when you want to complain, they look down their noses at you.
- They bring you the bill, and take their own time coming to collect the money.
- They are not prompt with service but expect a hefty tip.

38. The above list is 'The top complaints about _____.'
    (a) chefs   (b) servers
    (c) waiters   (d) customers

39. How is the bread that they give you?
    (a) Moist   (b) Fresh
    (c) Soft   (d) Old

40. According to this list, though they are lethargic to serve you, they expect a _____ reward.
    (a) Small   (b) reasonable
    (c) big   (d) little

41. They bring you the menu and then _____.
    (a) Disappear (b) go back stage
    (c) evaporate (d) camouflage
42. When you want to call them, they _____.
    (a) smile at you
    (b) wave out to you
    (c) pretend not to notice
    (d) come over immediately
43. When you say something is badly prepared, they _____.
    (a) don't listen to you
    (b) blow their noses at you
    (c) start crying and sniffing
    (d) treat you as if you were inferior
44. The water they give you is _____.
    (a) Smelly (b) scented
    (c) expensive (d) cheap

SECTION-III : SPOKEN AND WRITTEN EXPRESSION

Choose the best option for each situation.

45. Sheila : _____
    Tina : Oh, I stayed at home and watched TV.
    (a) How was work yesterday?
    (b) What did you do all weekend?
    (c) Did you enjoy the beach?
    (d) Have you been sick?
46. Visitor : Can you tell me how to get to the bank, please?
    Policeman : _____
    (a) Go away, don't bother me now.
    (b) Turn left at the next traffic lights.
    (c) Where are you from?
    (d) It's to the north-east.

Choose the best option to complete the conversation from the options below.

Jim : Hi, Tara, _____ (47) _____ you're free tomorrow night.
Tara : I guess I am. _____ (48) _____
Jim : I've just got a couple of tickets for the new Dark Knight movie. Are you interested?
Tara : Definitely, _____ (49) _____.
Jim : _____ (50) _____. See you tomorrow then.

47. (a) Can you tell
    (b) I was wondering if
    (c) Will you be
    (d) Do you think if
48. (a) Why do you ask?
    (b) What's your problem?
    (c) I'm not sure.
    (d) Sorry, I'm not.
49. (a) Not this tim.
    (b) Thanks for inviting me.
    (c) I'm coming.
    (d) Sorry to disappoint you.
50. (a) No problem.
    (b) Not an issue.
    (c) Not again.
    (d) No hassles.

Answer Keys

Scan the QR Code to see the Hints and Solutions

Access Content Online on Dropbox: https://www.dropbox.com/scl/fi/x1il8nzpuzwm1qyz8yycu/NSO-01-Science-Olympiad-Hints-and-Solutions.pdf?rlkey=kzkx1753ie7dfs4rlkt3yo4pa&dl=0

SECTION 1: WORD AND STRUCTURE KNOWLEDGE

1. SPELLINGS AND COLLOCATIONNS

Answer Key

I

| 1. (b) | 2. (d) | 3. (c) | 4. (b) | 5. (c) | | | | | |

II

| 1. (a) | 2. (c) | 3. (b) | 4. (d) | 5. (c) | 6. (b) | 7. (d) | 8. (c) | 9. (d) | 10. (c) |
| 11. (a) | 12. (b) | 13. (c) | 14. (a) | 15. (b) | | | | | |

III

| 1. (a) | 2. (b) | 3. (b) | 4. (d) | 5. (d) | 6. (c) | 7. (d) | 8. (c) | 9. (b) | 10. (b) |

IV

| 1. (a) | 2. (c) | 3. (c) | 4. (b) | 5. (c) | 6. (a) | 7. (b) | 8. (a) | 9. (a) | 10. (c) |
| 11. (d) | 12. (c) | 13. (a) | 14. (c) | 15. (c) | 16. (b) | 17. (c) | 18. (c) | 19. (d) | 20. (a) |

HOTS

| 1. (a) | 2. (b) | 3. (c) | 4. (d) | 5. (b) | 6. (b) | 7. (a) | 8. (b) | 9. (c) | 10. (a) |

2. SYNONYMS, ANTONYMS, HOMONYMS AND HOMOPHONES

Answer Key

I

| 1. (a) | 2. (b) | 3. (d) | 4. (c) | 5. (a) | 6. (b) | 7. (a) | 8. (b) | 9. (b) | 10. (c) |
| 11. (c) | 12. (c) | 13. (a) | 14. (d) | 15. (c) | 16. (a) | 17. (b) | 18. (c) | 19. (c) | 20. (c) |

II

| 1. (a) | 2. (c) | 3. (b) | 4. (d) | 5. (b) | 6. (c) | 7. (a) | 8. (d) | 9. (b) | 10. (a) |

III										
1. (c)	2. (c)	3. (c)	4. (d)	5. (b)	6. (c)	7. (d)	8. (d)	9. (b)	10. (c)
11. (d)	12. (c)	13. (b)	14. (c)	15. (d)	16. (d)	17. (b)	18. (b)	19. (a)	20. (a)
IV										
1. (a)	2. (b)	3. (c)	4. (a)	5. (d)	6. (b)	7. (d)	8. (c)	9. (a)	10. (c)
11. (d)	12. (a)	13. (c)	14. (b)	15. (d)					
V										
1. (b)	2. (a)	3. (b)	4. (c)	5. (d)	6. (b)	7. (a)	8. (c)	9. (a)	10. (c)
11. (d)	12. (b)	13. (c)	14. (b)	15. (a)	16. (b)	17. (c)	18. (b)	19. (a)	20. (d)

HOTS

I										
1. (a)	2. (d)	3. (b)	4. (c)	5. (a)	6. (a)	7. (d)	8. (c)	9. (a)	10. (b)

II				
1. (a)	2. (c)	3. (a)	4. (b)	5. (c)

3. ANALOGIES

Answer Key

I										
1. (a)	2. (b)	3. (c)	4. (b)	5. (a)	6. (a)	7. (a)	8. (a)	9. (a)	10. (b)
11. (a)	12. (c)	13. (a)	14. (c)	15. (d)	16. (b)	17. (a)	18. (b)	19. (a)	20. (c)
21. (c)	22. (c)	23. (d)	24. (a)	25. (d)	26. (b)	27. (a)	28. (d)	29. (d)	30. (b)
II										
1. (c)	2. (a)	3. (d)	4. (b)	5. (a)	6. (b)	7. (a)	8. (a)	9. (c)	10. (b)

HOTS

1. (d)	2. (b)	3. (c)	4. (b)	5. (a)

4. ONE WORD

Answer Key

1. (b)	2. (a)	3. (d)	4. (c)	5. (b)	6. (a)	7. (c)	8. (b)	9. (d)	10. (c)
11. (a)	12. (c)	13. (d)	14. (d)	15. (a)	16. (c)	17. (b)	18. (d)	19. (d)	20. (b)

HOTS

1. (a)	2. (c)	3. (d)	4. (a)	5. (b)	6. (c)	7. (d)	8. (c)	9. (d)	10. (b)

5. PHRASAL VERBS AND IDIOMS, MODALS, WORD ORDER

Answer Key

I

1. (d)	2. (d)	3. (b)	4. (a)	5. (a)	6. (d)	7. (b)	8. (a)	9. (b)	10. (b)
11. (d)	12. (a)	13. (b)	14. (d)	15. (b)	16. (a)	17. (c)	18. (c)	19. (c)	20. (a)

II

1. (c)	2. (b)	3. (b)	4. (d)	5. (a)	6. (b)	7. (b)	8. (b)	9. (b)	10. (c)
11. (d)	12. (c)	13. (b)	14. (a)	15. (a)	16. (c)	17. (a)	18. (a)		

III

1. (a)	2. (b)	3. (d)	4. (b)	5. (d)	6. (c)	7. (a)	8. (c)	9. (b)	10. (a)
11. (d)	12. (c)	13. (a)	14. (d)	15. (a)	16. (b)	17. (c)	18. (d)	19. (c)	20. (b)

IV

1. (a)	2. (a)	3. (c)	4. (b)	5. (c)	6. (b)	7. (d)	8. (a)	9. (b)	10. (b)
11. (c)	12. (a)	13. (d)	14. (c)	15. (a)	16. (d)	17. (b)	18. (c)	19. (d)	20. (c)

HOTS

I

1. (a)	2. (a)	3. (b)	4. (c)

	II		
1. (b)	2. (c)		
	III		
1. (c)	2. (c)		
	IV		
1. (a)	2. (c)		

6. NOUNS AND PRONOUNS

Answer Key

I									
1. (d)	2. (a)	3. (d)	4. (b)	5. (a)	6. (c)	7. (b)	8. (b)	9. (c)	10. (a)
II									
1. (a)	2. (d)	3. (c)	4. (a)	5. (b)	6. (c)	7. (d)	8. (a)	9. (b)	10. (c)
III									
1. (a)	2. (d)	3. (b)	4. (c)	5. (b)	6. (d)	7. (b)	8. (c)	9. (a)	10. (b)
IV									
1. (b)	2. (b)	3. (c)	4. (d)	5. (a)	6. (c)	7. (d)	8. (a)	9. (b)	10. (c)
V									
1. (a)	2. (b)	3. (c)	4. (c)	5. (a)	6. (c)	7. (b)	8. (c)	9. (a)	10. (c)
11. (c)	12. (c)	13. (b)	14. (c)	15. (d)	16. (c)	17. (b)	18. (a)	19. (b)	20. (d)

HOTS

I									
1. (a)	2. (b)	3. (b)	4. (a)	5. (b)	6. (b)	7. (a)	8. (a)	9. (b)	10. (a)
II									
1. (a)	2. (b)	3. (c)	4. (d)	5. (c)					

7. VERBS AND ADVERBS

Answer Key

I

1. (a)	2. (b)	3. (c)	4. (d)	5. (b)	6. (d)	7. (c)	8. (a)	9. (b)	10. (a)
11. (b)	12. (d)	13. (a)	14. (b)	15. (c)					

II

1. (a)	2. (c)	3. (d)	4. (a)	5. (a)	6. (a)	7. (b)	8. (a)	9. (c)	10. (c)
11. (d)	12. (d)	13. (c)	14. (a)	15. (d)					

III

1. (a)	2. (a)	3. (b)	4. (a)	5. (d)	6. (a)	7. (d)	8. (c)	9. (c)	10. (d)

IV

1. (a)	2. (b)	3. (d)	4. (c)	5. (b)	6. (a)	7. (b)	8. (d)	9. (c)	10. (b)
11. (c)	12. (a)	13. (d)	14. (b)	15. (d)					

V

1. (a)	2. (b)	3. (d)	4. (c)	5. (b)	6. (a)	7. (d)	8. (c)	9. (a)	10. (b)

VI

1. (c)	2. (a)	3. (b)	4. (d)	5. (a)	6. (b)	7. (c)	8. (d)	9. (b)	10. (c)

HOTS

I

1. (c)	2. (b)	3. (a)	

II

1. (b)	2. (d)	3. (b)	

III

1. (a)	2. (b)	3. (d)	4. (a)

8. ADJECTIVES

Answer Key

I

| 1. (a) | 2. (c) | 3. (a) | 4. (c) | 5. (b) | 6. (c) | 7. (b) | 8. (a) | 9. (c) | 10. (c) |

II

| 1. (c) | 2. (a) | 3. (c) | 4. (c) | 5. (b) | 6. (a) | 7. (b) | 8. (c) | 9. (b) | 10. (b) |
| 11. (c) | 12. (c) | 13. (a) | 14. (b) | 15. (c) | 16. (b) | 17. (c) | 18. (b) | 19. (b) | 20. (a) |

HOTS

| 1. (b) | 2. (c) | 3. (c) | 4. (b) | 5. (d) |

9. ARTICLES AND PREPOSITIONS

Answer Key

I

1. (a)	2. (d)	3. (b)	4. (a)	5. (b)	6. (b)	7. (b)	8. (d)	9. (a)	10. (c)
11. (c)	12. (a)	13. (c)	14. (c)	15. (d)	16. (d)	17. (c)	18. (b)	19. (c)	20. (b)
21. (a)	22. (d)	23. (d)	24. (d)	25. (a)					

II

1. (b)	2. (c)	3. (c)	4. (b)	5. (d)	6. (d)	7. (a)	8. (d)	9. (a)	10. (b)
11. (c)	12. (d)	13. (a)	14. (b)	15. (d)	16. (a)	17. (b)	18. (c)	19. (b)	20. (c)
21. (c)	22. (c)	23. (a)	24. (c)	25. (d)	26. (c)	27. (c)	28. (a)	29. (c)	30. (d)

HOTS

| 1. (a) | 2. (b) | 3. (b) | 4. (c) | 5. (b) |

10. CONJUNCTIONS AND PUNCTUATIONS

Answer Key

I

| 1. (a) | 2. (d) | 3. (b) | 4. (c) | 5. (a) | 6. (d) | 7. (a) | 8. (b) | 9. (a) | 10. (d) |

II

| 1. (a) | 2. (d) | 3. (a) | 4. (b) | 5. (d) | 6. (b) | 7. (c) | 8. (b) | 9. (c) | 10. (d) |

III

1. (b)	2. (a)	3. (c)	4. (d)	5. (d)	6. (c)	7. (b)	8. (c)	9. (a)	10. (c)
11. (a)	12. (d)	13. (b)	14. (b)	15. (c)	16. (c)	17. (b)	18. (a)	19. (b)	20. (a)
21. (a)	22. (c)	23. (d)	24. (c)	25. (c)	26. (d)	27. (b)	28. (c)	29. (c)	30. (d)

IV

| 1. (a) | 2. (b) | 3. (d) | 4. (c) | 5. (d) |

HOTS

| 1. (d) | 2. (d) | 3. (b) | 4. (b) | 5. (d) |

11. TENSES

Answer Key

| 1. (a) | 2. (b) | 3. (b) | 4. (c) | 5. (a) | 6. (c) | 7. (c) | 8. (c) | 9. (d) | 10. (d) |
| 11. (c) | 12. (b) | 13. (b) | 14. (c) | 15. (b) | | | | | |

HOTS

| 1. (a) | 2. (a) | 3. (a) | 4. (c) | 5. (c) | 6. (b) | 7. (c) | 8. (a) | 9. (b) | 10. (d) |
| 11. (d) | 12. (a) | 13. (a) | 14. (a) | 15. (c) | 16. (c) | 17. (a) | 18. (d) | 19. (b) | 20. (a) |

12. VOICES AND NARRATION

Answer Key

I

1. (c)	2. (b)	3. (a)	4. (c)	5. (b)	6. (c)	7. (d)	8. (b)	9. (b)	10. (b)
11. (a)	12. (b)	13. (c)	14. (d)	15. (b)	16. (b)	17. (b)	18. (d)	19. (b)	20. (d)
21. (a)	22. (a)	23. (a)	24. (b)	25. (c)	26. (d)	27. (d)	28. (c)	29. (d)	30. (b)
31. (a)	32. (b)	33. (a)	34. (c)	35. (b)	36. (b)	37. (b)	38. (a)	39. (a)	40. (b)

II

1. (a)	2. (d)	3. (a)	4. (d)	5. (a)	6. (d)	7. (b)	8. (a)	9. (c)	10. (a)
11. (c)	12. (b)	13. (c)	14. (d)	15. (b)	16. (c)	17. (d)	18. (a)	19. (b)	20. (c)
21. (a)	22. (d)	23. (b)	24. (c)	25. (d)	26. (a)	27. (b)	28. (c)	29. (a)	30. (a)
31. (a)	32. (c)	33. (b)	34. (a)	35. (d)	36. (a)	37. (b)	38. (b)	39. (a)	40. (c)

HOTS

| 1. (d) | 2. (d) | 3. (d) | 4. (d) | 5. (d) |

13. VOCABULARY

Answer Key

I

| 1. (a) | 2. (c) | 3. (b) | 4. (d) | 5. (a) | 6. (b) | 7. (d) | 8. (c) | 9. (a) | 10. (b) |

II

| 1. (a) | 2. (c) | 3. (b) | 4. (d) | 5. (a) | 6. (c) | 7. (a) | 8. (b) | 9. (d) | 10. (b) |

III

| 1. (c) | 2. (b) | 3. (a) | 4. (d) | 5. (b) | | | | | |

HOTS										
1. (c)	2. (b)	3. (a)	4. (d)	5. (b)	6. (a)	7. (a)	8. (d)	9. (b)	10. (a)

SECTION 2: READING COMPREHENSION

1. READING COMPREHENSION - I

Answer Key				
I				
1. (c)	2. (a)	3. (d)	4. (c)	5. (a)
II				
1. (c)	2. (a)	3. (b)	4. (d)	5. (d)
III				
1. (a)	2. (d)	3. (b)	4. (b)	5. (a)
IV				
1. (b)	2. (a)	3. (c)	4. (d)	5. (a)
V				
1. (b)	2. (d)	3. (a)	4. (b)	5. (b)
VI					
1. (a)	2. (c)	3. (b)	4. (d)	5. (b)	6. (b)
VII				
1. (a)	2. (d)	3. (c)	4. (b)	5. (a)
VIII				
1. (b)	2. (a)	3. (d)	4. (c)	5. (c)

2. READING COMPREHENSION - II

Answer Key

I

1. (i) (a)	(ii) (c)	(iii) (d)	2. (i) (b)	(ii) (c)	3 (i) (d)	(ii) (a)	4. (i) (d)
5. (i) (c)	(ii) (c)	6. (d)	7. (d)	8. (b)			

II

1. (b)	2. (a)	3. (c)	4. (b)	5. (d)			

III

1. (d)	2. (a)	3. (c)	4. (a)	5. (d)	6. (a)		

IV

1. (c)	2. (d)	3. (a)	4. (c)	5. (b)			

V

1. (b)	2. (a)	3. (d)	4. (c)	5. (b)			

VI

1. (b)	2. (c)	3. (a)					

SECTION 3: SPOKEN AND WRITTEN EXPRESSIONS

Answer Key

1. (a)	2. (a)	3. (c)	4. (d)	5. (b)	6. (c)	7. (a)	8. (b)	9. (d)	10. (c)
11. (d)	12. (a)	13. (b)	14. (c)	15. (b)	16. (a)	17. (a)	18. (d)	19. (a)	20. (a)

MODEL TEST PAPER–1

Answer Key

I	1. (b)	2. (a)	3. (c)	4. (c)	5. (b)
II	1. (d)	2. (c)	3. (b)	4. (d)	5. (b)
III	1. (b)	2. (d)	3. (a)	4. (d)	5. (d)
IV	1. (c)	2. (d)	3. (a)	4. (a)	5. (b)
V	1. (b)	2. (a)	3. (c)	4. (c)	5. (b)
VI	1. (a)	2. (c)	3. (d)	4. (a)	5. (a)
VII	1. (c)	2. (c)	3. (a)	4. (c)	
VIII	1. (c)	2. (c)	3. (c)		
IX	1. (b)	2. (a)	3. (c)	4. (a)	5. (b)
X	\multicolumn{5}{l}{1. Because he thought that he was free to do what he liked.}

X
1. Because he thought that he was free to do what he liked.
2. A man walking behind him objected.
3. The gentleman argued that the was free to do what he liked.
4. No, the other was not satisfied.
5. He said that the gentleman can enjoy his rights and freedom if they do interfere with others rights and freedom.

Achiever's Section

1. (b)	2. (d)	3. (d)	4. (c)	5. (b)	

MODEL TEST PAPER – 2

Answer Key

1. (c)	2. (b)	3. (a)	4. (d)	5. (c)	6. (a)	7. (d)	8. (a)	9. (b)	10. (c)
11. (d)	12. (a)	13. (c)	14. (b)	15. (d)	16. (a)	17. (c)	18. (a)	19. (b)	20. (d)
21. (b)	22. (c)	23. (d)	24. (a)	25. (a)	26. (b)	27. (c)	28. (a)	29. (c)	30. (c)
31. (b)	32. (b)	33. (a)	34. (b)	35. (a)	36. (a)	37. (d)	38. (c)	39. (d)	40. (c)
41. (a)	42. (c)	43. (d)	44. (c)	45. (b)	46. (b)	47. (b)	48. (a)	49. (b)	50. (a)

Appendix

There are different organizations that conduct these examinations and covering all of them is not needed as the focus should be to understand the main type of exams conducted. They are similar for these organizations with the difference being the change in name of the exam.

\multicolumn{3}{c}{Science Olympiad Foundation (SOF)}		
S. No.	Name of Exam	Grade
1.	National Science Olympiad (NSO)	Class 1-10
2.	National Cyber Olympiad (NCO)	Class 1-10
3.	International Mathematics Olympiad (IMO)	Class 1-10
4.	International English Olympiad (IEO)	Class 1-10
5.	International Commerce Olympiad (ICO)	Class 1-10
6.	International General Knowledge Olympiad (IGKO)	Class 1-10
7.	International Social Studies Olympiad (ISSO)	Class 1-10
\multicolumn{3}{c}{Indian Talent Olympiad (ITO)}		
S. No.	Name of Exam	Grade
1.	International Science Olympiad (ISO)	Class 1-12
2.	International Math Olympiad (IMO)	Class 1-12
3.	English International Olympiad (EIO)	Class 1-12
4.	General Knowledge International Olympiad (GKIO)	Class 1-12
5.	International Computer Olympiad (ICO)	Class 1-12
6.	International Drawing Olympiad (IDO)	Class 1-12
7.	National Essay Olympiad (NESO)	Class 1-12
8.	National Social Studies Olympiad (NSSO)	Class 1-12
\multicolumn{3}{c}{EduHeal Foundation}		
S. No.	Name of Exam	Grade
1.	Eduheal International Cyber Olympiad (ICO)	Class 1-12
2.	Eduheal International English Olympiad (IEO)	Class 1-12
3.	National Interactive Math Olympiad (NIMO)	Class 1-12
4.	National Interactive Science Olympiad (NISO)	Class 1-12
5.	International General Knowledge Olympiad (IGO)	Class 1-12
6.	National Space Science Olympiad (NSSO)	Class 1-12

Humming Bird Education		
S. No.	Name of Exam	Grade
1.	Humming Bird Commerce Competency Olympiad (HCC)	Class 1-12
2.	Humming Bird Cyber Olympiad (HCO)	Class 1-12
3.	Humming Bird English Olympiad (HEO)	Class 1-12
4.	Humming Bird General Knowledge Olympiad (HGO)	Class 1-12
5.	Humming Bird Hindi Olympiad (HHO)	Class 1-12
6.	Humming Bird Mathematics Olympiad (HMO)	Class 1-12
7.	Humming Bird Science Olympiad (HSO)	Class 1-12
8.	Humming Bird Aptitude and Reasoning Olympiad (ARO)	Class 1-12
9.	Humming Bird Spelling Competition (Spell BEE)	Class 1-12
10.	Humming Bird Language Olympiad	Class 1-12
International Assessments for Indian Schools (IAIS) (MacMillan and EEA Collaboration)		
S. No.	Name of Exam	Grade
1.	IAIS Maths Olympiad	Class 3-12
2.	IAIS ScienceOlympiad	Class 3-12
3.	IAIS English Olympiad	Class 3-12
4.	IAIS Digital Technologies Olympiad	Class 3-12
SilverZone Foundation		
S. No.	Name of Exam	Grade
1.	International Informatics Olympiad	Class 1-12
2.	International Olympiad of Mathematics	Class 1-12
3.	International Olympiad of Science	Class 1-12
Unified Council		
S. No.	Name of Exam	Grade
1.	Unified Council Cyber Exam	Class 1-12
2.	Unified International English Olympiad.	Class 1-12
3.	Unified International Mathematics Olympiad (UIMO)	Class 1-12
Unicus		
S. No.	Name of Exam	Grade
1.	Unicus Non-Routine Mathematics Olympiad (UNRMO)	Class 1-11
2.	Unicus Mathematics Olympiad (UMO)	Class 1-11

3.	Unicus Science Olympiad (USO)	Class 1-11
4.	Unicus English Olympiad (UEO)	Class 1-11
5.	Unicus Cyber Olympiad (UCO)	Class 1-11
6.	Unicus General knowledge Olympiad (UGKO)	Class 1-11
7.	Unicus Critical Thinking Olympiad (UCTO)	Class 1-11
CREST (Online Mode)		
S. No.	Name of Exam	Grade
1.	Mathematics (CMO)	Classes KG-10
2.	Science (CSO)	Classes KG-10
3.	English (CEO)	Classes KG-10
4.	Computer (CCO)	Classes 1-10
5.	Reasoning (CRO)	Classes 1-10
6.	Spell Bee Summer (CSB)	Classes 1-8
7.	Spell Bee Winter (CSBW)	Classes 1-8
8.	Mental Maths (MMO)	Classes 1-12
9.	Green Warrior Olympiad (GWO)	Classes 1-12

How To Apply?

Anyone willing to participate in the Olympiad exam can follow these steps to apply for the exam:

- ☞ Log in to the official website of the conducting organization.
- ☞ Find the Registration Option to register
- ☞ Fill up the details such as Student Name, Parent Name, School Name, Class, Postal Address, E-mail Address, Password, etc.
- ☞ Select the subjects you want to apply for. Pay the necessary registration fees and you are done.
- ☞ You will receive necessary details on your email id.

There are no minimum marks required by the Olympiad conducting organizations to apply for the exam.

Awards

Based on the organization rules, students as well as schools participating in these exams are awarded with several recognitions based on the marks they score.

www.ingramcontent.com/pod-product-compliance
Lightning Source LLC
Chambersburg PA
CBHW080921180426

43192CB00040B/2608